WHAT JUST HAPPENED?

How To Bounce Back in Life so You Can Do More, Have More, and Be More

Written by:

Mr. Jimmy Burgess

This book is dedicated to my wife Tasha Grames Burgess. You have loved and supported me through it all. You have proven again and again that you meant what you said on our wedding day. You meant it when you said you would be true in good times and in bad. You meant it when you said for richer or for poorer. You meant it when you said in sickness and in health. Thank you for always making my job as your husband much easier than your job as my wife.

An excellent wife who can find? She is far more precious than jewels. Proverbs 31:10 (ESV)

TABLE OF CONTENTS

Introduction

"A few years' experience will convince us that those things which at the time they happened we regarded as our greatest misfortunes have proved our greatest blessings."

George Mason

Why does life have to be so hard? Is this all life has to offer? Will this pain and struggle ever end? Why can't I catch a break? Why me?

Have you ever asked yourself any of these questions? We all do from time to time. We all face struggles. We all have setbacks in life that seem insurmountable. There have been certain moments in my life when things were going great, and then *boom*—everything seems to blow up. At these moments I have wondered, *What just happened?* After working extremely hard for over a year for a hefty raise that did not come, I wondered, *What just happened?* When the real estate market collapsed around 2008, and my personal finances collapsed, I was left wondering, *What just happened?* When the doctor told me I had a mass on my false vocal cord at thirty-five years old, I wondered, *What just happened?* Has there ever been a time when you wondered, *What just happened?*

Sometimes it takes unexpected and unwanted circumstances to move us to action. I am very proud of the young lady my teenage daughter is becoming. However, like with most teenagers, sometimes it takes a jolt or something a little scary to happen in order for her to be moved to action. I will say, for example, "Please take your plate to the sink," and she will barely acknowledge me. Then, again, I will calmly say, "Please take your plate to the sink." "Okay," she'll say. Five minutes later, I will walk into the kitchen and see her plate still on the table. By then my blood will be boiling. Then my eyes will turn red, my head will spin around a few times, and I'll yell, "If this plate is not in the sink in two seconds,

I am about to move some furniture around in here!" She will look at me in the sarcastic way that teenage girls do and say, "What just happened?"

Unfortunately it sometimes takes something scary, unwanted, and unexpected to move us as adults to action as well. For me it has taken drastic situations to motivate me to change areas of my life that needed to be changed.

Everybody faces struggles and setbacks in life. The difference is that some people bounce back, and others stay in their struggles. After bouncing back from setbacks in my life, I had a few people ask me how I was able to not only bounce back but to do it very quickly. This question was something I had never thought about before. This led me on a search for why some people bounce back and others seem to stay in their struggles. After a few years of research, I realized that the same steps I used to bounce back have been used for thousands of years. I uncovered a seven-step process that results in a life of more, and many times situations and struggles can change to the positive very quickly. These steps aren't just something I read about or think might work for you. These are the seven steps that I know will work for you if you apply them. They changed my life, and I believe with all my heart that they can change yours as well.

Jack Canfield (motivational speaker and author) compares being successful to knowing the combination to a lock. If you know the combination, it will always open. The key to success and, in this case, bouncing back is knowing the combination to the lock. In this book, I will share the combination numbers that have worked for me personally and for others throughout history to bounce back from life's struggles.

The following is a breakdown of the chapters and steps you will learn to help you bounce back from whatever life has thrown at you:

- Chapter 1, "My Story. Out of the Ashes"—This chapter will give you a glimpse into how quickly things can change in both directions. You'll learn how shifting your focus through one small step can change everything in an instant.

- Chapter 2, "Understanding the Platforms of Change. How to Find Balance"—This chapter will show you the three platforms that direct your life. You'll learn how to create a life of balance that will take you from where you are to where you want to be.

- Chapter 3, "Step 1: Admit and Take Ownership of Your Actions. How to Move from Victim to Victor"—This chapter will break chains that have been holding you back. You will learn how to let your past (which you cannot change or control) go and focus on your future (which you completely control).

- Chapter 4, "Step 2: Flood Your Mind with Positivity. How to Inspire Yourself to Greatness"—This chapter will teach you how to create contagiously positive situations. You'll learn how to change your mind, which, in turn, will change your life.

- Chapter 5, "Step 3: Believe to Achieve. How to Believe Yourself to the Next Level"—This chapter will teach you how to change your beliefs in a way that will make it inevitable that your future will be better than your past. You'll learn how to transform your belief system into the fuel that motivates you to do more, have more, and be more.

- Chapter 6, "Step 4: Find a Mentor or Coach. How to Gain Wisdom and Vision through Accountability"—This chapter will teach you how to create an environment of accountability that will push you to higher levels than you thought possible. You'll learn how to put the right people around you to create laser-like focus that leads you to your dream life.

- Chapter 7, "Step 5: Set the Course of Your Life with Goals. How to Create a Step-by-Step Guide to Your Dreams"—This chapter will teach you how to create your dream future by breaking it down into daily steps. You'll learn how to develop a plan that flips everything so that life reacts to you instead of you reacting to life.

- Chapter 8, "Step 6: Change Your Way to Greatness. How to Make Changes That Transform Your Life"—This chapter will teach you how to turn generational curses into generational blessings. You'll learn how to make changes that will move your life from good to great.

- Chapter 8, "Step 7: Turn Your Mess into Your Message. How to Create Your Enduring Legacy"—This chapter will teach you how to turn your struggles into your strengths. You'll learn how to transform yourself into the person you were created to become.

Whether your struggle is financial, relational, physical, or all of the above, these seven steps can move you from where you are today to where you were destined and created to go. You were created for more: more peace, more joy, more love, and more of everything this life has to offer. This is your moment to find hope, a plan of action, and excitement about your future.

I know that I don't have it all figured out, and I still have daily struggles. However, one day I woke up and I was more content and happy than ever before in all areas of my life, and I asked myself, "What just happened?"

Let's get started on your transformation!

Chapter 1

My Story
Out of the Ashes

"No one said that life was going to be easy; life is the hardest thing there is, but you learn through it all. Whether you're making mistakes or living in the happiest moment in your life, there will be difficulties and you have to believe in yourself that you can succeed through it all. No one is holding you back but yourself."

Author Unknown

My palms were sweating as I shook hands with the bank's CEO. We were meeting in his top-floor office overlooking a golf course with the Gulf of Mexico in the distance. The end-of-the-year evaluation was the time when raises were given. Finally, my patience would pay off.

I had been working for the bank for a little over a year. Prior to taking the job with the bank, I was a Realtor™ with my family-owned real estate company. Due to my contacts from the real estate business, I played a decent-sized role in the growth spurt the bank had seen over the past year in their commercial real estate portfolio. I was told by numerous bank employees that I was adding more value to the bank's bottom line and at a quicker pace than anyone before me. I was excited about my future with the bank.

Three months prior to the end-of-the-year evaluation, I had requested a meeting with the CEO. At that meeting, I laid out the business I had brought to the bank in the form of fee income, ongoing interest income, and new strategic relationships in less than a year. I showed him how I had generated income for more than double the amount of my annual salary. I also laid out a plan of action to increase my output. I then asked for a raise. I was told the bank only gave raises at the end-of-the-year evaluations. He told me he appreciated everything I was doing and to be patient because the bank was going to take care of me.

So, as I sat down for this end-of-the-year evaluation, I was nervous but excited to see how the bank was "going to take care of" me. He began by telling me what a great job I had done. He told me I had been a big part of the commercial loan portfolio growth. He seemed excited to tell me that the board had agreed to give me a raise that was higher than what they usually gave a first-year employee.

I could feel my chest puffing out as my anticipation grew. He reiterated, "We rarely give this much, but…" My heart was beating so fast that I wondered if he could see it through my shirt. He then paused, smiled big, and said, "We're giving you a five-percent raise."

At that moment, it was like I had been physically punched in the stomach. Just that week, I had closed one loan that had upfront fee income to the bank four times the amount of the annual raise he proposed to give me. In my mind I thought, *Are you kidding me?* Apparently my facial expression didn't hide my displeasure because he quickly said, "We don't give raises to first-year employees bigger than five percent. This is a great raise."

At that moment, I took a quick mental trip to Crazyville. Maybe it's just me, but have you ever felt so unappreciated that you wanted to pick up a chair and throw it through a picture window in a penthouse office? I snapped back to sanity, stood up, stuck my hand out to shake his, and simply said, "Thank you." He said, "Jimmy, just be patient; the bank is going to take care of you in time." That one sentence was like an arrow in my heart as I left his office. As the elevator door closed, I wondered if life was meant to be lived patiently waiting for someone else to take care of me and my family.

When the elevator doors opened, I went straight out to my car and drove the short distance to a spot overlooking the beach. I rolled my windows down, hoping the cool December breeze and sound of lapping surf would calm my anger. The raise, which I viewed as a slap in the face, wasn't the only reason for my anger. I was thirty-three years old at the time. Have you ever awakened one day and thought that you would have accomplished more by now? That's where I was!

I always believed that by then (age thirty-three), I would have been in a better position financially than living paycheck to paycheck. I believed I would have accomplished more. I thought all I had to do was work hard and the "American dream" would be mine. This end-of-the-year evaluation made me realize that I didn't want to wait for others to give me something. This evaluation made me mad enough to do something about my life. Sometimes anger is the fuel for change. In this case, it was for me. I decided as I sat in my car overlooking the gulf that I would never let someone else tell me how much I was worth again. I decided to never let someone else put a cap on my income. Finally, I was mad enough to change!

That night, I began reflecting on my life. I remembered something I heard Brian Tracy (a motivational speaker and author) say one time about work and savings, and I measured myself by it that night. Since my high school graduation, I had been to college for four years and worked hard for eleven years. Due to mostly matching retirement plan contributions, I had a grand total in retirement accounts of about fourteen thousand dollars and one thousand dollars in a savings account. All of the sudden it hit me. In the past fifteen years since I left high school, I had accumulated a grand total of fifteen thousand dollars (of which over 90 percent couldn't be touched until I was almost sixty years old). This meant I had basically worked the past fifteen years for room and board plus eighty dollars per month. If someone had offered me a job that paid room and board plus eighty dollars a month, I would have told them they were crazy! Yet I had basically done it to myself for the past fifteen years.

I began to ask myself a few questions. Was room and board plus eighty dollars a month all life had to offer? Was watching the clock all day just waiting for five o'clock going to be my routine for life? I knew I couldn't just go through the motions anymore. I had to make a change, but I wasn't sure how. I wanted passion in my life. I wanted excitement. I wanted to make a difference. Even though I didn't know how, I made a decision not to accept mediocrity for the rest of my life.

Within a few days, I read a passage in the Bible from Mathew 7:7 that said "seek and you will find." This was like an earthquake in my soul. I began to seek knowledge. I knew that if I was going to change, I had to change from the inside out. I needed to put positive in if I expected to get positive out. I began reading inspirational books. I would listen to positive, inspirational, and motivational speakers in my car on my forty-minute commute to work and home in the evenings. Even though my situation didn't change immediately, I could feel changes beginning to simmer below the surface. My outlook on life was changing. Hope began to overtake worry. Thankfulness began to conquer concern. Positivity showed up instead of negativity.

While listening to a Zig Ziglar (an author, salesman, and motivational speaker) CD in my car one day, he said something I had heard him say dozens of times before. He said, "If you will help enough other people get what they want, then you will get what you want." Even though I had heard it many times before, this time I was ready to receive it. I realized that my passion was helping other people get what they wanted. I shifted my thinking from what I wanted and began focusing on what others wanted. This shift in thinking changed everything.

Over the next few months, I was still working at the bank assisting mostly wealthy bank customers with business loans and real estate development loans. I was seeking knowledge and shifting my focus to helping others get what they wanted. Now, when my phone rang, I began to view each call as a way to help others. After solving their needs, I would usually ask them if I could ask them a couple of questions. The first was always, "How did you get started?" This is a great question to ask people. What I realized is that every person has a starting point and something that turns the light on for them. Most of the people I spoke with loved what they did. I got great insight on persistence and self-belief. It seemed like, in most cases, the money just followed their passion and hard work.

The second question I would ask was, "Where do you see opportunities now?" Most all said their business. I later realized it was because their business was what they loved. But the main thing I heard from the majority was that it didn't really matter what business it was but that it was something they loved to do. Many of them told me of failures they had in other businesses because it wasn't something they were passionate about.

The third question was, "What is an ideal opportunity or project you are looking for right now that could enhance your business?" I found it alarming how quickly they all answered this question. I got many different answers to this question; however, they were all very specific. I asked one of the men how he was able to tell me what he was looking for so quickly. He said, "I focus an hour a day trying to find it." I realized they were all focused on specific items to enhance their businesses.

The final question I asked was, "If I found what you were looking for, could I be a part of it?" Some said, "It depends on what you bring," and others said, "Yes." Many of them asked if I was looking to leave the bank. I would always answer the same way: "Just like you, I am always looking for opportunities."

Even though nothing happened for a few months, I knew momentum was building. I was compiling a list of wants and needs for each of my bank customers. The funny thing was that because I was asking these questions of my bank customers, they began to see me differently than just a commercial loan officer. My referrals began coming in like crazy, and my bank loan portfolio was growing faster than ever. This was despite the fact that my mind was constantly searching for knowledge and opportunities rather than bank loans.

Then one day it happened. One of my best bank customers just laid me out. I called him about a loan I was working on for him. At the end of the call, he asked me if I had seen any opportunities in the market like he mentioned he would be interested in a few months earlier. I said, "No, but I am looking." He then said the words I needed to hear: "Jimmy, unless you swing the bat, you're never going to hit the ball. I can't say yes if you never show me anything." Wow, that one statement pierced my heart and mind.

That statement was exactly what I needed to hear. I knew that all the knowledge in the world was useless if it was not accompanied by action. I pulled out the list I made of projects/businesses people told me they would be interested in hearing about. I made up my mind that I was going to find something that I could present to somebody within the next two weeks.

A couple days later, I got a call from a group that wanted to finance a subdivision that had been divided into lots twenty years prior, but the roads and water/sewer had not been installed. Like everyone, they wanted to finance the development with very little money down. The projections they provided included a price per lot that I felt was conservative for the hot real estate market we were experiencing. After going through all their projections, I realized it was evident that the bank would require them to put down more money upfront than they wanted to.

I decided not to call them back with the news that we couldn't finance the project until the next morning. I knew there had to be an opportunity to help them, but I just needed to think about it for a while. That night, I focused on their main need, which was how to get this project done with as little money upfront as possible. I thought about how other developments had gotten off the ground with lower amounts of upfront money. I sat up most of the night thinking of options, and finally one hit me.

The next morning, I set up a meeting with a few of the partners, which included an attorney and a couple of real estate brokers. We decided to meet at the office of one of the real estate brokers. As we walked into the expansive office, my heart was racing. It was time to put all the knowledge I had been learning to work.

I started by telling them I had some good news, and I had some bad news. Then I began, "First the bad news. The bank is not going to be willing to finance the project without a substantially larger amount of upfront money." Dejected, one of the partners asked, "What's the good news?" Then I started my pitch: "I may have found a way that you can do the project with no upfront money or loan." This got their attention. I continued, "Even though the roads and utilities are not in place, the lots are recorded and could be sold as is." One of the real estate brokers said, "Nobody is going to buy a lot that doesn't have the roads and utilities in place for top dollar."

"You are right," I said. "But instead of selling the lots for full market value, why not sell them at a discount with the understanding that cash generated from the lot sales would be put in escrow [a place where it can only be used for a specific purpose] for all needed improvements to the subdivision to be completed within a specific time? The discounted lot prices would basically be giving the cash you would have paid the bank for closing costs and interest to the purchasers. So it would be a wash to your bottom line."

I saw lights beginning to go off because they had not thought of this before. I continued, "Also, the prices you have in your projections for lot prices appear to have been put together six months ago. The market has moved at least twenty percent higher since then, and I believe the lots could be sold right now, as they are, with the plan I just laid out at your projected price. Based on my projections, you could sell about sixty percent of the lots in this subdivision simultaneously (the same day as you purchase the whole project) and have enough cash to buy the land, escrow funds for all improvements, and have one million dollars plus forty percent of the lots left over."

The attorney chimed in, "I could have a contract like this drawn up with these terms fairly quickly, but I am just not sure people will buy the lots without the infrastructure in place for those prices." Before the real estate brokers could say anything, I jumped in head first. "For bringing this option to you, I want the ability to prove to you that the lots can be sold for these prices. I would like the ability to get a group of these lots under contract within forty-eight hours of you getting me a usable contract [I still had my real estate license active]. I would like a five-percent commission on the purchase price of this group of lots."

The main real estate broker partner then said, "I know the market is hot, but I am just not completely convinced we can sell the lots that quickly. I say we draw up a contract that Jimmy can use and give him the forty-eight hours to see if it is possible." Everybody agreed.

As I pulled out of the parking lot, I finally allowed myself to get excited. But now was when most people would panic. I had to sell the lots, or the whole idea was useless. However, I had been asking people for months what type of projects they would be interested in if I found them. Many of my bank customers were contractors. Due to the market heating up, many of them mentioned a desire to buy lots in new subdivisions with early/lower pricing to build speculation homes (homes to sell). That morning, I called a couple of the builders before my meeting with the development group. I told them what I might have and asked them if they would be interested. They all said they would be extremely interested. I figured if they were then others would be as well.

Around noon that day, the attorney sent over the contract to use. Within a couple of hours, I was in front of the land with an aerial map on the hood of my truck offering the lots to the contractors on my list who had told me this was what they were always looking to buy. Every single one I called wanted at least one lot, and many wanted multiple lots. Within three hours, I had the group of lots they gave me the ability to sell under contract and at the development group's full asking price. I knew it would take about ninety days for the lots to close and that I should never count my chickens before they hatched. However, that evening driving home, I realized that when/if these lots closed, I would earn double my annual bank salary in one day.

I couldn't wait to share what happened with the bank customer who had encouraged me to take action. When I told him about it, his response was not what I expected. He said, "That's great that you made the commission. But the idea you gave them put millions of dollars in their pocket. If you would have asked them upfront for a small part of ownership in the development for bringing them an idea that made them millions and saved them a ton of time then they would have been stupid not to give it to you." This is yet another reason it is so important to spend time with people who have a bigger vision of life than we do. Now I could see even bigger opportunities.

Since I wanted to make sure the lots were going to sell before I moved on from the bank, I continued to look for opportunities in the coming weeks. I was approached by an old friend about a development he was looking to finance. After talking with him, I began to see the potential to help in a bigger way than banking. After I asked some additional questions, he told me his ideal situation would be to take on some partners that put the cash up to get a loan on the development. Learning from the lot sales, I asked if I could have a small percentage ownership in the development group if I found equity partners for him. He quickly agreed, and I pulled out my list to see who had mentioned wanting to be a part of a commercial/condo development project.

After pitching the project to four different people who all said no, I was more convinced than ever that this project had a tremendous amount of potential. I was running out of people to pitch it to, so I called the man who had encouraged me to take action. I told him I had something I wanted his opinion on that wasn't exactly what he told me he was looking to do, but I saw potential. He agreed, and I went to his house along with the developer. In less than two hours, he had agreed to do the development project, and we were off to the races!

One month later, I met with the bank CEO again in his top-floor office. This time I thanked him for the opportunity to work at the bank and shared with him the opportunities I had with the development projects. I tendered my resignation and saw my life change financially very shortly after that meeting. Within one year, my annual bank salary became my monthly income. Within two years, my annual bank salary was my average biweekly earnings. I worked extremely hard over the next few years and made a pile of money. But... Why does there always have to be a "but"?

But things began to change in 2005. The real estate market came to a screeching halt. However, the market wasn't the only thing that had changed. Somewhere along the way I began to feel like I had made it. My ego began to swell. I stopped being a seeker and started being a know-it-all. I was hard to live with during this time, especially for my wife because I thought it was all about me. Physically I was mess. I could see it all beginning to slip away, but my ego wouldn't let me put a stop to it. I made bad decision after bad decision because I thought I was bullet-proof.

Within a couple of years, I was sitting with my wife in federal bankruptcy court with five hundred dollars in cash to my name. It was humiliating and humbling. How could I let this happen? How could I put my wife and family in this position? How could I be so stupid? I had a lot of negative self-talk going on during this time.

Winding up in bankruptcy court didn't happen overnight, and the slow tail-spin into the ground was painful. During this time, financial problems weren't all I was facing. The lifestyle I had been living and the stress of bankruptcy landed me in a hospital with a health scare at thirty-five years old. Although my marriage was not in question, I knew that my selfishness and ego were planting seeds that could harden my wife's heart toward me. My life was a hot mess!

One day I read an article about people who bounced back after bankruptcy. The article detailed how Henry Ford, Abe Lincoln, and Walt Disney had all been through bankruptcy before changing the world with their creativity and leadership. The article discussed how they all came out on the other side of bankruptcy stronger because they never forgot that bankruptcy couldn't take their most valuable assets, which were their minds and their work ethic. All of a sudden it hit me. I had been so busy over the past eighteen months focusing on not losing everything financially that I stopped seeking knowledge and growing. I was living a fake life because I was worried about what other people might think of me. I stopped growing, and we all know that if you are not growing, you are dying.

I thought back on what got me moving the first time. I remembered that I focused on what others wanted or needed. I remembered how I read and listened to positive and motivating books and CDs. Finally, I remembered that what I enjoyed most was helping others get what they wanted. For the past eighteen months, all I had focused on was how bad things were in my life. It has been my experience that what we focus on expands. The more I thought about how bad things were, the worse they got. I began to change my thoughts. I began to focus, as much as possible, on the positives in my life. I began searching for opportunities again.

I wish I could say things changed overnight, but they didn't. There are always consequences for our actions, and unfortunately it took a couple years for us to reach the point where we ended up filing for bankruptcy. However, over the six months prior to filing, I began to prepare myself for life after bankruptcy. I was burned out on real estate, and I knew that I needed to find something else. I needed to find something I would enjoy doing, and the money would follow. My bankruptcy attorney gave us a date that was about six months out when we would run out of the cash we had remaining and be able to file our bankruptcy. I became extremely focused on creating something new that would generate an income.

Once again, I remembered the scripture that basically said "seekers find." I began to seek opportunities. One day in late 2008, I ran across an article on cnbc.com that gave five ways to make some quick cash. One of the ways was to host a gold party. A gold party is basically where a host invites friends over to his home to sell their broken, unwanted, or out-of-style gold jewelry. The gold party representative separates the jewelry by carat purity, weighs it out, and pays the seller in cash a portion of the gold melt value. The party host then receives 10 percent of the total amount purchased for hosting the party. The article said these parties were spreading across the country like wildfire.

After reading that article, I figured if the host made 10 percent then the gold party company was doing even better. I realized that everybody in America was going through the "great recession" in late 2008. I understood that what everybody wanted or needed at that time was extra cash. I thought about how much fun it would be to pass out cash in a party atmosphere. This sounded like my dream job. Two problems were I didn't have any cash to buy gold with, and I didn't know a thing about jewelry. My dad's friend lived a few hours away from me and had been in the jewelry business for about twenty years. I called my dad and ran the gold party company idea by him. He thought it was a great idea, so I asked him to give me his friend's phone number.

I called the jeweler and asked him if he had heard of a gold party before. He had not, but he thought it was a great idea after I explained it to him. I asked him if he would be interested in coming over to my house and buying if I hosted a party for some of my friends. He agreed, and with fewer than eight people there, he paid out a little over two thousand dollars for the gold. Out of the few people at our home that night, three of them wanted to host their own parties. The party was a blast, and the gold party idea appeared to have legs.

That night we were excited about the possibilities. I knew it was now or never to make my pitch to the jeweler and my dad (they had decided to partner up). I was transparent with the jeweler. I told him I was roughly three months away from filing bankruptcy. I was willing to do all the work of booking the parties, marketing, and follow-up for the next few months for very little compensation if he would be willing to train me on how to value jewelry items and run the business. Basically, I was looking for an internship in the jewelry business. I also asked them to consider loaning me enough money to start my own gold party company if they saw that it was profitable and they had confidence in me.

They agreed, and I began promoting the gold parties with a vengeance. We ended up having over forty parties in those ninety days. He taught me a tremendous amount about jewelry during that time, and I felt confident enough to start my own company. Once the bankruptcy was filed, I established my gold party company fairly shortly thereafter. They loaned me a portion of the profits they made since starting their gold party company, and I went to work. Within the first year in business, and one year removed from sitting in bankruptcy court with five hundred dollars in cash to my name, the gold party company had gross income before expenses and taxes in excess of a million dollars. Gross income was nowhere near my take-home income after all expenses, but the heat of paying the bills was removed.

When we are in storms, it is sometimes hard to realize that we are being molded for something greater to come. Living in a rural community, I sometimes have the opportunity to see things that others may not see. We lived next door to a small family farm a couple of years ago. On two sides of our home, there were pastures where our neighbor had livestock. When summer arrived, our neighbor spent time away for a number of months. Since he knew he was going to be gone, he sold all his animals before leaving. Since the pastures were untended, they grew all summer and winter uninhibited. This normally well-kept pasture grew grass, weeds, and briers during this time. Over that short period of time, the weeds and briers began to take over the pasture (as weeds and briers always do when left unattended). There was less and less life-giving grass as the weeds and briers began to overtake the pasture.

One morning in the early spring, my neighbor had the forestry department at his home. They took a tractor and disked a line around the outside fence and set fire to the pasture. What a mess this made. The smoke filled the air, and when the fire was done, the pasture that was so beautiful just a year ago was scorched black. It smelled like smoke for a week and looked horrible. Then a rain came. Within a few days, green shoots started popping up all over this black and barren pasture. Within a week, the blackness of the fire faded into the greenest pasture for miles. Not only that, the green was life-giving and desirable grass. The green, life-giving grass always comes back first. The weeds and briers will eventually come back, but my neighbor tended to his field and kept them at bay. The neighbor now knew where they were most likely to start popping up, and he paid special attention to those areas to make sure his past problem areas were not able to take root again.

Looking back on the financial firestorm in my life, I saw it was mostly due to the weeds and briers in my life that I allowed to grow unattended. The firestorm is a trying time. When the fire is the hottest and you don't think you can take anymore, that is the time when the deepest-rooted briers and weeds are burned away. These are some of the toughest times in life. Even after the firestorm ends, there is a time when you are scorched and the blackness of the fire looks hopeless. *But rain always comes!* Goodness springs forth from darkness. You come out of the fire with new growth and a new understanding of your weak areas. The weeds and briers always try to come back. But, because of the fire, you know where these areas are and prepare for their arrival. By knowing where they are, you can remove them before they grow to a point where they can produce seeds that begin to take over other areas of your life.

If you are in a firestorm now, understand that out of this, new and better growth will come. Know that rain always comes. Understand that the greatest time for new growth is right after the rain when the scorched ground is its ugliest. Understand that firestorms refine you for new and better growth. Instead of wallowing in the ashes of the firestorm, pray for rain. When the rain comes, fertilize the new growth. Nurture it and treasure it. No matter how hot the fire you are in or have been in has gotten, stay encouraged. You are being refined and prepared for a great life.

After coming through the bankruptcy and bouncing back, I began to wonder how and why we were able to bounce back while others were still struggling. I began to study other people throughout history who had bounced back from setbacks. I began to see patterns. I began to see clear steps and processes that almost every person who bounced back went through. I began to realize that I was identifying the combination numbers that could help others unlock the chains that were holding them back. I began to feel the need to share this information with others. I believe with all my heart that your reading this book right now is not by accident. The mere fact that you are reading this book proves that you are seeking. As I have stated before, seekers always become finders.

I realized a few things since I emerged from my financial storm. What I believed would be one of the worst things that could happen to me turned out to be the best thing that ever happened to me. I am thankful for the blessings I have now more than ever before. I have the best relationship I have ever had with my wife and children. I am in the best physical shape of my life, and I am more connected with my God than ever before. I am a better person now than I was before. I am happier and more focused on serving others than ever before. To put it another way, it took my losing everything financially to gain everything in my life that money couldn't buy.

No matter where you are today, you are only a few decisions away from changing your thoughts, which will ultimately change your situation. You are not a victim. You can't control your past, but you have complete control of your future. Become a seeker. Become an inspiration to others. Become a fighter that will fight for your future and not accept mediocrity anymore. This is your time and this is your year to be an agent of change. You have been gifted with the power to create your perfect life. It is time to awaken the greatness inside you that has been waiting patiently for you to unleash it. Now is the time!

At the end of each chapter, you will find a set of steps that will lead you to your purpose. For some it will happen quickly, and for others it will take time. However, you will succeed if you never give up. Stop beating yourself up and speaking negatively to yourself. Today is a new day. Today is your day to change the trajectory of your life.

QUESTIONS TO ASK YOURSELF:

1. Am I feeding my mind positive food or negative food?

2. What do I love to do?

3. What are the needs or wants that I can help others fulfill?

4. Am I choosing to be bitter or choosing to get better?

5. What can I do to get excited about my future?

ACTION STEPS:

1. Set aside a minimum of twenty minutes a day to read or listen to positive and motivating books or speakers. This may be while you are driving, when you first wake up, or right before bed. Whenever works best for you, just do it.

2. Make a list of five things you enjoy doing. Do at least one of them each day.

3. Make a list of five needs or wants you see around you. Help someone else with at least one of these wants or needs each day.

4. Write down five goals you want to accomplish in the next week (they might be small, but they will get momentum moving). Examples could be losing two pounds this week, organizing your desk or something else in your life that is cluttered, catching up with an old friend with whom you have lost contact over the years, writing a love note to your significant other, writing a note to your kids telling them what you are proud of that they do, packing a lunch for work to save some money, etc.

5. Become a seeker. Spend at least ten minutes a day searching online for opportunities to get better.

Chapter 2

Understanding the Platforms of Change
How to Find Balance

"When you know better, you do better."

Dr. Maya Angelou

Change can happen when new information is presented. Eric Thomas (CEO and founder of Eric Thomas and Associates) puts it this way: "Information changes situations." Identifying an area of weakness and making a small change in one area can create momentum that leads to change in another area. Each of us operates our lives from three different platforms. They are our minds, our bodies, and our souls. The critical part to realize is that if you are weak in one area, it can spread like cancer to the other areas. It is also critical to realize that if you strengthen one area, it can lead to strengthening the other areas. Momentum is instrumental in creating your desired life. We are always changing in one direction or the other. We are either growing or we are dying. We can, in times of transition, be growing in one platform and dying in another. However, growth and death cannot operate simultaneously forever. Sooner or later one will become dominant and overtake the other in all areas of your life.

Let's examine the three platforms. The soul is the control center platform. It is our connection to our Creator. It is where all goodness in us originates. Hope resides in the soul. It is where our desires are generated. It is where we are different from anyone else. The soul is our rudder in life. It directs us in the direction of goodness and purpose. The soul does not change but only increases in influence as we work to understand our Creator.

Each of us has certain combinations of traits and gifts that no one else in history has ever possessed. We all have certain activities we love, and we are just naturally good at these activities. These are the things that no one ever had to teach us to do; we just knew. These unique gifts are a part of who we are and reside in our soul. The soul is the area where, as you strengthen it, you will begin to become less self-focused, more compassionate, and you will become magnetic.

Haven't we all been around a person who just lights up a room when he or she enters it? When you spend time with that individual, you feel better about yourself and your situation. These are typically people who are tapped in to their Creator and their individual purposes in life. You leave their presence, and you want whatever it is that they have going on in their lives.

I am not speaking of religion but rather of living a purposeful life, doing what you individually were created to do—a life focused on maximizing your God-given talents. If you are struggling in this platform now, odds are you have more than likely been solely focused on your own problems. That self-focus has made you unable to help others around you in their times of need, which is a purpose we are all created to fulfill.

The second platform is our minds. The mind is our platform of thoughts. Our minds are not structured to decipher good from bad but rather to amplify what we consume. Think of it as if you were a computer. Your soul is like the hardware that has given you a blueprint of certain gifts. However, your mind is more like the software. The old saying about computers, "garbage in, garbage out," also applies to your mind. If you are constantly putting in negative content, you will constantly see negative results and situations. However, if you are constantly putting in positive and uplifting content, you will see positive results and experience uplifting experiences.

Your mind is where your beliefs reside. The good news is that you may not be able to control what is going on around you, but you can control your thoughts and how you react to them. Ultimately, our thoughts create our environment. Bob Proctor (author of the book *You Were Born Rich*) puts it this way: "Thoughts become things." It is essential that you realize the power of your thoughts. It is critical that you mind your thoughts and flood your brain with positive messages.

Odds are if you are struggling in this platform, you have been putting more negative thoughts in your mind over time than positive thoughts.

The third platform is your body. The body is the platform of action. You can think all the positive thoughts you want, but if you do not use your body to take action then it is irrelevant. Without good health, the other two platforms are limited in their effectiveness. If you are healthy, you become more effective because you have more energy. If you work toward keeping your body in optimum condition then your whole outlook on life changes. You begin to think long term rather than short term.

Whereas the states of your soul and mind are not visible, the state of your body's physical condition is constantly in front of you. At a minimum every morning and night, when you brush your teeth, you see yourself in the mirror. When you look in the mirror, you either tell your mind that you look horrible, you look great, or that you are improving. Isn't it clear how empowering or destructive this self-talk can be in all areas of your life? Odds are if you are struggling in this platform now, you are not in peak physical condition or in the process of getting in better shape.

Balance in all three platforms is the key to long-term success. Short-term success can be achieved by excelling in one or two areas. However, if you allow weakness in any of the three platforms to fester, it will eventually lead to destruction. One of the most public examples of this is Tiger Woods. Physically he has always been in optimum shape. His mind has been able to create incredible focus on the golf course. Prior to his scandal in 2009, he was able mentally to call upon past triumphs and fill his head with positive thoughts that created positive results in stressful situations on the golf course. There was no one stronger in golf mentally or physically.

Every once in a while, Tiger would undermine his own integrity when he let profanity fly out of his mouth without regard for the impressionable youth around him or watching him on television. He undermined his own character when he mistreated reporters. His ego prevented him from apologizing for any of it.

Eventually, the truth came out. He had cheated on his wife with dozens of women. His moral compass had apparently been numbed over time. He appeared to be so disconnected from his soul (his life rudder) that it cost him everything that money couldn't buy. It cost him his marriage. It cost him his family. It cost him his reputation. It cost him friends and their respect. It cost him his confidence. It also reportedly cost him hundreds of millions of dollars in a divorce settlement and lost sponsorships.

When he returned to tournament golf, you could tell that the public meltdown on one platform (soul) had spilled over to the other platforms. For years he struggled with closing out and losing tournaments that he would have won easily before the scandal. Physically he began to hit golf shots that were so bad he never would have dreamed of hitting them before. Mentally you could see his confidence was not what it used to be. Only time will tell if he is able to fully recover from these costly decisions.

The good news for Tiger, and for all of us, is that if we are weak in any area, it can be renewed and changed. The soul can be realigned through prayer, study, and shifting from self-focus to a focus on the needs of others. I have a group of verses from the Bible that are promises from God that I repeat to myself in times of distress. Something moves in my spirit when I hear a verse like: "'For I know the plans I have for you,' says the Lord. 'They are plans for good and not for disaster, plans to give you a future and a hope'" (Jeremiah 29:11).

Realignment with your soul can also begin by shifting your focus from your daily struggles to a heart of thankfulness. In times of distress, I take out a sheet of paper and list fifty people or things I am thankful for in my life. I also try to start every day off with a time when I reflect on three or four things that I am thankful for that day. I begin each day by rolling out of bed. When my first foot hits the floor, I say, "Thank," and when my second foot hits the floor, I say, "you." I do this every day. Some days it is easier than others, but starting my day out with thankfulness creates positive momentum for my day. The shift to thankfulness is a big step in coming into harmony with your spirit and your purpose.

Your mind can be renewed by simply pouring positive messaging into it. It may take some time, but if you consistently stretch your mind with new knowledge and inspiration then you will begin to feel the momentum of change bubbling in your mind. You will begin to see the good in people and situations rather than the bad. You will begin to smile more and laugh more.

Music and art can also play roles in renewing your mind. Appreciating and fully examining a great painting can inspire your mind positively as well.

Music can stir the emotions and open your mind to inspiration. If you surround yourself with great things then you will begin to see and expect great things in your life.

Your body can be changed visibly in a rather short period of time if you have been living a sedimentary life. Small changes can lead to momentum for larger changes. Did you know that science has discovered that a large part of our bodies is renewed every seven years? When cells die, new ones are created. This means you can physically change not only your appearance but your life expectancy by recreating a healthy body.

Start out slowly and push yourself to get better and stronger every day. Cut down or out destructive habits and unhealthy foods. You don't have to do it all at once but set small goals so that you will see progress. By achieving goals and seeing small results, you will be motivated to make additional changes in your lifestyle as needed.

Success is not easy. If it were, everybody would be successful. However, if you are willing to put in the hard work and honestly evaluate yourself then I promise you can succeed. The key to prolonged improvement in the three platforms is consistency. If you consistently work on all three platforms then your life will change for the better.

It may seem that we drifted away from the action steps you need to bounce back financially. However, understanding the psychology of change is the foundation you must possess before change will come. In the coming chapters, I will share with you the time-tested steps that people have used throughout history to bounce back from all kinds of setbacks. These are the exact steps I used. These steps are not just something I read about or something that I think will work. These are steps that I know will work for you if you are committed to change because they worked for me.

You may feel that your life has been out of control. At this moment, I want you to realize that you control your destiny. No longer are you going to be a victim of your circumstances. Your future is dependent on you, and you have the power to create the future you desire and are destined to see. Now it's time to roll up our sleeves and get started!

QUESTIONS TO ASK YOURSELF:

1. Right now, am I growing or dying spiritually, mentally, and physically?

2. Am I focused on myself or others?

3. Do I feed my mind a majority of positive messages or negative messages?

4. Am I getting stronger or weaker physically every day?

5. What inspires me?

6. What will my ideal life look like when I bring all three platforms into balance?

7. What is the one thing I can do to get better today?

ACTION STEPS:

1. Every morning when you wake up, say, "Thank" when your first foot hits the floor and "you" when your second foot hits the floor.

2. Make a list of fifty people/things you are thankful for in your life and read it each morning for a month as soon as you wake up.

3. Change the background photo on your computer to a photo of a beautiful piece of art or inspiring quote.

4. Don't watch the news for one month (bad news sells, and that is all they report these days). Instead, read a good book. Listen to inspiring music or a motivational CD.

5. Break a sweat every day for thirty days.

6. Remove one destructive food or drink a day. In other words, if you usually drink two carbonated drinks a day, just drink one. Or if you usually have a hamburger at lunch, substitute a lean protein sandwich like turkey or chicken breast on whole wheat bread.

7. Once you see results in any area, increase the intensity and number of activities to see more results.

Chapter 3

Step 1: Admit and Take Ownership of Your Actions

How to Move From Victim to Victor

"If you could kick the person in the pants responsible for most of your troubles, you wouldn't be able to sit for a month."

Theodore Roosevelt

Victims blame others for their situations while victors take responsibility and learn from their mistakes. Blame has become a sport. Political parties blame each other for problems, and no one works on solutions. Excuses seem to have replaced action. However, blaming others and not taking responsibility is nothing new.

As a matter of fact, one of the first stories ever reported speaks of a man and a woman who couldn't take ownership of their mistakes. The story goes that Adam and Eve ate fruit from the one tree they were told by God to leave alone. When God asked Adam if he had eaten of the tree that He told him not to eat of, what was his response? He said, "It wasn't me. It was that woman that you gave me." He blamed everybody possible at that time. He blamed God for giving him the woman and the woman for giving him the fruit. So if you have been blaming your situation on others, you aren't alone and your actions are not a new thing.

When my finances were tail spinning out of control, I blamed the economy. I blamed clients that filed frivolous lawsuits. I blamed partners in the developments. I blamed clients who wouldn't fulfill contracts they had agreed to and on and on and on. Things finally began to change when I took ownership of my mistakes. Even though there were some things that were out of my control, the majority of my issues came from poor decisions on my part.

I saw the red flags during the contract negotiations with the person who would later file a frivolous lawsuit against me. But I overlooked the character of this person, despite the red flags, due to the amount of money I would make. I allowed a salesperson with a low moral character to stay in my office. I let him stay because he was generating a lot of income instead of removing him before he and his clients ultimately caused major problems. Instead of putting cash away for a rainy day, I was more interested in making it rain (not exactly like that, but you get the idea about where I was mentally).

As in most cases when things began to unravel financially, they also began to unravel in my health. Most people don't realize this, but the opposite of disease is at ease. As you can imagine, during this time, I was anything but at ease.

I developed a cough around January of 2006 that ended with me losing my voice for over three months. At the beginning, I blamed the cough on the weather we had experienced. One day it would be thirty degrees and then seventy-five degrees the next. When I lost my voice and went to the local doctor, he prescribed cough medicine that kept me loopy and in bed for a couple of weeks. I still didn't have a voice three weeks later, so I made an appointment with a pulmonologist to check out my lungs. He performed a bronchoscopy. He told me I just needed to rest and take additional medication for my voice to return. He told me there was an abrasion on my false vocal cord that appeared to be due to the coughing. He didn't seem concerned, so I wasn't.

Three weeks later, I still didn't have a voice, and I asked (actually my wife asked because I could only whisper) to be referred to the best voice person the pulmonologist could find. That resulted in my being referred to Dr. Ossoff of the Vanderbilt University Hospital in Nashville, Tennessee. He turned out to be one of the most world-renowned voice specialists in the country.

Let me give you a glimpse into my state of mind over the three months that I did not have a voice. As my financial world around me was collapsing, I could not physically drive to my office due to the medication I was taking. I could not communicate with my clients, employees, or development partners on the phone because my whisper was not loud enough to be understood. I was basically out of pocket and bedridden for three months when I desperately needed to be working to save my family financially. I was angry at the doctors for not fixing me. I was frustrated that I could not physically do the things needed to run my businesses on a daily basis. Every day, I woke up thinking that this would be the day I would get my voice back and I could get back to work. But days turned into weeks, and weeks turned into months.

I was so busy focusing on blaming others that I completely missed the root of the problem. The root of the problem was that since the age of eighteen, I had been a smoker. When things got more stressful (and they had been very stressful at that time), I smoked more. I was also twenty-five to thirty pounds overweight at that time. I was embarrassed by my smoking because in my heart of hearts I knew it was an ignorant habit. But it was a habit that I seemingly could not quit. Therefore, I tried to hide it from certain people. I tried to hide it from my kids. I attempted to hide it from people that I thought would judge me. As a side bar, if there is anything in your life that you feel you have to hide from anybody then it needs to be removed!

I quit smoking about a month prior to going to Vanderbilt because of the coughing and how painful it was to smoke. At that time it was extremely difficult but necessary. However, I was still angry that the doctors had not fixed this problem yet. Even worse, at this time I was angry at God. My conversations with God then involved my asking Him why He was punishing me (that is the way I viewed it even though it wasn't punishment). I wondered why God would make me go through this when I was a pretty good guy. I wondered why I was being punished when I read my Bible occasionally, I attended church, and I tithed. How could God punish me and not that guy over there who acts the way he acts? So that was my mentality as I walked through the doors of Dr. Ossoff's office. I was angry, frustrated, and blaming other people and things for my poor health.

The walls of Dr. Ossoff's office are covered in gold records and letters of thanks from every country music singer you can imagine. Johnny Cash, George Jones, Reba McIntyre, and Faith Hill are just a few of the artists that had letters framed on the wall thanking him for helping them with their voices. There was even a framed

People magazine with an article discussing how he treated Bill Clinton when he had voice problems while serving as president. Now my anger turned into cockiness. Finally I was going to get my voice back. This doctor was the best in the world. He would give me the magic pill, and I could get back to work.

Including Dr. Ossoff, three doctors did complete external and internal exams from my stomach up. By the time they finished their tests at around three-thirty that afternoon, I was physically exhausted. My wife and I sat in the exam room along with Dr. Ossoff and one of his interns. They had a video of one of the scopes they ran down my throat playing on a flat-screen TV on the wall. They were talking to each other, but I couldn't understand what they were saying due to the amount of medical terms they were using. He froze the video, leaned forward in his chair, and pointed to the screen. He said, "Jimmy, these are your vocal cords here, and these are your false vocal cords here. Can you see a difference in your left false vocal cord and your right false vocal cord?" I whispered yes because I still didn't have a voice. Then in a serious voice he said, "That is what we call an abnormality or mass on your left false vocal cord. We would like to get an MRI done immediately to see what it might be."

He continued talking for another five to ten minutes about what it might be and what it might not be, but I really didn't hear anything he said. I don't know if you have ever heard a doctor tell you that he sees an abnormality in your body, but, at thirty five years old, it shook me to my core. I didn't show any emotion sitting there with that doctor and my wife, but I wasn't angry at God anymore. I was scared. I was as scared as I had ever been.

They immediately sent me to another part of the hospital for the MRI. I remember being in that cold, sterile room where the MRI was about to be performed. The nurse put the IV in my arm for the dye. She told me that my family was in the waiting room and that she would be in the adjoining room while the MRI was running. As she left the room, I remember hearing that big steel door shut behind her. Ka-boom! At that very moment, I felt completely and utterly alone. I remember lying flat as I heard the whirling sound of the MRI begin to gather images of my neck and throat. For the first time since I had lost my voice, I felt a tear roll down my right cheek. I realized that I had no control over this situation at that moment.

I am what many would consider a control freak. If there is a problem, I want to know what it is so that I can fix it and move on to the next issue. I realized at that moment that, including me, there was no one in this world who could fix this issue. The only one who could fix it was the one I had been angry with just hours before. Although I felt alone just seconds before, I now realized that I wasn't alone. God had been there the entire time. Now with tears running down both my cheeks, I began to pray. "Lord, I am sorry for the ways that I fall short of the man you created me to be on a daily basis. I need you now more than ever. I pray that if you see fit to heal me, you open my eyes to the blessings I have been taking for granted."

I don't know how long the MRI continued, but it didn't seem long before the nurse came back in the room and told me I was good to go. I asked for a moment to compose myself before going to meet my wife, mom, and stepfather, who were in the waiting room. I didn't tell anyone about my time in that MRI for a few months, but I walked out of that room a changed man.

A few hours later the doctor called, and he said it appeared to be a clear cyst. Now that they had a baseline on its size, they wanted me to do voice therapy and a new medication for a month before returning to Nashville. When I returned to Nashville in a month or so, they said they would make a decision on whether they needed to take a biopsy or perform surgery. The next morning back at my home, my wife woke me with the new medication, and she smiled at me as she left the room. It was as if cataracts had been removed from my eyes, and I realized how blessed I was to have a wife who meant it when she said "in sickness and in health." She meant it when she said "for richer or for poorer." I realized how much she meant to me and how much I had been taking her for granted.

That afternoon as I was sleeping in my bed (as I had most afternoons over the past few months), I woke up to the sound of the front door opening. It was my two daughters coming home from school. They crawled up in the bed with their sick father, and I had one arm wrapped around each of them. They laughed and giggled, and so did I for one of the first times in months. I realized how blessed I was to be able to spend that time with them. After all, these two girls had not seen their dad for days and weeks at a time. It wasn't because I was off on some extravagant trip. It was because I was out doing what the world told me I should be doing to get ahead financially. Most days I left for work long before they were awake and got home from work long after they had gone to bed. For days at a time the only interaction we had was my kissing them on the forehead while they slept. However, as we laughed together in the bed that afternoon, I realized how blessed I was to be their father.

Over the next few weeks, I admitted to myself that I was the one to blame for losing my voice. I was an overweight smoker who was blaming everybody else for my health and financial problems. Once I admitted it to myself and took ownership of my responsibility, my whole mindset began to change. Instead of being a victim of my circumstances, I began to search out ways to improve my situation. Instead of excuses, I began to search for solutions. Instead of playing defense on my heels, I began to shift to my toes and play offense. One month later, with my voice restored, I returned to Dr. Ossoff's office in Nashville. After many tests, he told me the cyst was completely gone and that I was making a miraculous recovery. He didn't know how true that was, not just physically but in all areas of my life.

By the time I began to repair my body physically, work on my soul connection, and change my mind to a positive mindset, unfortunately it was too late to save my financial situation. Although I ended up having to file for bankruptcy, I was on my way to restoration. It all started when I took ownership of my mistakes. I evaluated my mistakes and attempted to burn the lessons learned deep into my mind to make sure I never allowed the same snake to bite me twice. Yes, there were instances when people did things that I could not control. However, if I dug a little deeper, I would almost always find poor decisions I made that allowed them to be in a position to negatively affect my life. Admitting and taking ownership of your actions is the first step in every restoration program, and it is your first step to restoration as well.

Sometimes things happen that we have no control over. Although we cannot always control what happens to us, we can control how we react to it and how we make changes in our lives to minimize the chances of them returning later. It is time for you to stop blaming others for your situation. Take complete ownership. Until you admit your responsibility, you cannot learn from your mistakes because you still don't view them as your mistakes. Until you evaluate your mistakes and learn the lesson that you need to learn, you will not be able to move forward.

Break the bondage of the victim mentality. There is freedom in taking responsibility for your past and taking control of your future. I love the lyrics from the song "You Are More" by Tenth Avenue North that say, "You are more than the choices that you make. You are more than the sum of your past mistakes."

Today is a new day. There is nothing you can do to change your yesterdays, but the decisions you make today will determine your tomorrows. Have you ever wondered why the rearview mirror in a car is so small and the windshield is so large? It is because we are made to look where we are going and not where we have been. Yes, we occasionally need to glance back to make sure nothing is coming up behind us. But one of the quickest ways to cause a wreck is to stare into your rearview mirror for an extended period of time. Looking back only distracts you from where you are headed. Tear your rearview mirror off if need be. If you are going to bounce back, you must focus on your future instead of your past.

The sun rises just after the darkest part of the night. No matter how dark it seems right now, the sun is about to rise for you. You are not a victim. You are a victor. It is time for you to be the windshield instead of the bug. Flood your mind with positives to flush out the negatives like worry, doubt, and fear. Embrace hope. Embrace love. Embrace peace. Embrace your destiny!

QUESTIONS TO ASK YOURSELF:

1. Am I blaming others for my mistakes?

2. Do I feel like a victim or a victor?

3. Do I have any activities that I hide from others?

4. Do I have any destructive habits?

5. Did I do anything today that my future self will thank me for?

ACTION STEPS:

1. Make a list of people and things you have blamed. Draw an X through each of them and write to the side of them how you allowed the mistake to happen.

2. Write out a lesson you learned from each of the situations or people that you have blamed in the past.

3. Do a Google search for help groups to assist you in removing any destructive habits. Then take action!

4. Stop waiting for other people to make your situation better. If it is financial restoration you need, get a part-time job on top of your full-time job. If it is physical restoration you need, develop a diet and exercise plan. If it is spiritual restoration you need, study and pray. Do something today to start momentum in the right direction.

5. Either tell in person or write a note thanking four people who have been supportive of you when you needed them most. Amazingly, it will do more for you than it will for them.

Chapter 4

Step 2: Flood Your Mind with Positivity
How to Inspire Yourself to Greatness

"Change your thoughts, and you change your world."

Dr. Norman Vincent Peale

Positive thoughts are the seeds of change. If you are going to change your situation, you must first change your thoughts. Our thoughts become our beliefs, and our beliefs lead to action. In order to calibrate your mind to greater possibility and results, you must begin by feeding it positive food.

The concept of the farmer reaping what he sows has been around forever. Let's take, for illustrative purposes, a farmer who plants peanut seeds. He diligently cares for the seeds that he sowed. He fertilizes them, he waters them, and he makes sure the weeds and pests do not harm them. When it comes harvest time, he storms into his house and slams the door. When his wife asks him what is wrong, he responds, "I wanted potatoes, but when I turned the ground, there were peanuts."

This sounds ridiculous. How could the farmer really think that he was going to reap anything other than what he sowed? That's a great question. Now let me ask you another one. How is that any different than when we constantly feed our minds negative thoughts like worry, self-doubt, anger, bitterness, and jealousness and expect to magically reap positive results? An apple tree will always bear apples no matter how much we may want peaches. In order to change what we reap, we must first change what we sow.

For a few years I lived it up at the pity party. I not only attended, but I brought the "whine" and cheese. During this time I lived by the saying, "If you don't have anything nice to say, sit by me." Being around other people who were struggling was comforting. It was not motivational, but it was comforting because I wasn't alone. Have you ever noticed that people are contagious?

We all know people who say they are always sick and guess what: they are always sick. If you spend time with them, you will eventually start being sick as well. Spend time with a person who eats unhealthily and you will eventually eat unhealthily as well. How about your friends who drink excessively? Spend some time with them and see if you don't begin to do what they do.

Jim Rohn (an entrepreneur, author, and motivational speaker) taught that we are the average physically, mentally, financially, and spiritually of the five people with whom we spend the most time. This means if you are the smartest one of your friends then you need to get some new friends! If all your friends lead unhealthy lives then chances are your health will suffer. If all your friends believe that God or the world is out to get them then it will be difficult for you to not begin to believe that way. When I first began my process, I didn't know that many positive people that I could spend time with personally. So, instead of the physical person, I spent hours with motivational speakers through their products. I consumed their books and their audio programs. I bought their training programs, and I spent more time with them than anybody that I knew personally. If you don't have positive people around you now, spend time with positive authors and motivational speakers through their products. Eventually your transformation will draw other positive people to you.

The good news is that contagiousness works both ways, whether people have negative or positive characteristics. If the five people you spend the most time with eat healthily and exercise, odds are that you will become healthier. If you spend time with people who are successful, you will begin to speak and act in similar ways as them, which will result in your success. If you spend time with people who believe that God is for them and not against them then you will begin to believe the same way. If you and your spouse spend time with other couples that work on their marriages and are happy, your marriage will improve. If you want a certain result, spend time with people who have already gotten the desired result. I promise you that the result will come to you.

There was one particular day when my life was melting down that I will never forget. I was having lunch with a group of eight guys who worked in the same general area as me. One of the guys was telling a story about how drunk he had been the night before. Another guy at the table was having an affair. One of the other guys was on unemployment. He wasn't ashamed of it either. He said he had paid in for years, and he figured it was time he got something back. They were all laughing at all the stories and seemingly having a good time when all of a sudden I felt ill. I told the guys I didn't feel good, paid my bill, and hurried out of the restaurant.

A question popped into my head as I got outside: *Are these guys who you want to become?* This hit me like a Mike Tyson punch to the jaw, and I verbally said out loud, "No." This was a turning point for me. I made a decision to surround myself with positive people whenever possible. I made a decision to spend time with as many good husbands as I could so that I would be a better husband. I made a decision to spend time with good fathers so that I could become a better father. I made a decision to spend time with achievers and not deceivers. I wanted to be around people who inspired me instead of people who discouraged me.

I began flooding my mind with positive messages. I would listen to CDs from motivational speakers and biographies of inspirational people everywhere I went. I consumed business and inspirational books. I was hungry for knowledge, and the more I consumed, the hungrier I got. I began taking time to do things that inspired me. I would go to the beach with my family to watch the sunset. My family and I went to art festivals on weekends and walked around looking at fine art. We attended outdoor music events. None of these activities cost a penny but they inspired me and brought a smile back to my face.

All of a sudden the seeds of positivity that I was sowing began popping up through the ground. My relationship with my wife and family began getting stronger. My health began improving as I began to broaden my knowledge of healthy living and how it plays a role in everything we do. Although we were still struggling financially, I began to see opportunities instead of obstacles. I began to have hope instead of worry. I began to see the potential for abundance instead of lack in all areas of my life. Although my financial situation on the outside was not showing it yet, I knew I was different on the inside. Although it may take time to come out of your struggle, when you change from the inside, you can't stop it from manifesting on the outside.

Not only are people contagious, but we are, in a sense, magnetic. We draw others to us that are similar to us. This has been true our entire lives. If you aren't sure about this then just think back to your high school lunchroom. Think about how the jocks sat together. The popular kids sat together. The nerds sat together. No one ever had to tell people where to sit; we were just naturally drawn to the people like us. It is the same today.

That was why I was so alarmed and felt physically ill that day at lunch with that group of guys I mentioned above. I didn't belong with that group, but something inside me was sliding in that direction or I wouldn't have been there. I knew that if I was going to attract positive people, I needed to become a positive person. I knew that if I wanted to attract inspirational people then I needed to become an inspirational person. If I wanted to have people around me who were growing then I needed to be growing.

At that time, I began to realize that there are basically two kinds of people: people who are just surviving and people who are thriving. As you read the examples and differences of these two groups of people, ask yourself which one you are right now.

1. People who just *survive* go through life daily trying to make it through another day. People who *thrive* go through life excited about what each day holds for them to experience.

2. People who just *survive* have jobs they hate where they watch the clock to see how much longer they have until they can quit working each day. People who *thrive* have jobs they love where they watch the clock to see how much time they have until they have to quit.

3. People who just *survive* blame their bad health on having bad genes. People who *thrive* exercise and eat right so they can wear designer jeans.

4. People who just *survive* gossip so they can feel better about themselves. People who *thrive* have enough self-confidence to compliment others so that others can feel better about themselves.

5. People who just *survive* complain about how bad the future looks. People who *thrive* take action steps to ensure that tomorrow is even better than the great day they had today.

6. People who just *survive* aimlessly wander through life. People who *thrive* have clearly set goals and a daily action plan for how to achieve their goals.

7. People who just *survive* work hard. People who *thrive* work hard and smart.

8. People who just *survive* curse the darkness in the world. People who *thrive* carry a candle into the darkness.

Seek inspiration, and you will find it. Become a positive person, and you will attract positive people around you. Create an outbreak of positivity that cannot be controlled. It is irrelevant what your past or your present looks like. Where you are headed in the future is what is important. If you plant the seeds of positive thinking in your mind, you will be amazed by the harvest you will reap.

QUESTIONS TO ASK YOURSELF:

1. What one thing is the biggest source of negative thoughts in my life?

2. Are the people I spend time with helping me grow or die?

3. Have I been reaping what I have been sowing?

4. Have I done anything that could be considered planting positive seeds lately?

5. Is there something or someone in particular that is holding me back from being positive?

ACTION STEPS:

1. Listen to motivational CDs or books while you are in your car. If you have others with you, use the Audible application on your phone with ear buds. A great book to start with is *The Power of Positive Thinking* by Dr. Norman Vincent Peale.

2. Find a church where the music and message inspire you.

3. Do whatever makes you laugh. If that is a funny movie then go. If it is a comedy club then go. Whatever it is, do it. Laughing always changes your outlook toward positivity.

4. Spend more time with positive people. Invite one positive person or someone who inspires you to lunch each week.

5. Smile at everyone you pass. Smiling is contagious, and it will also help you to move yourself into a state of positivity.

Chapter 5

Step 3: Believe to Achieve

How to Believe Your Way to the Next Level

"Whether you think you can or think you can't—you are right."

Henry Ford

What you believe about yourself is what you will become. Belief is one of the strongest emotions available to us. Belief creates action. Belief gives you the strength to persevere through disappointment and struggle. Belief gives you the ability to stay focused when distractions come. Belief is a fire in your belly that cannot be extinguished. Once you stop thinking you can do something and shift to believing you can do it, the outcome becomes "when," not "if."

What do you believe about yourself? Do you believe you were created just to go through the motions? Do you believe that your gifts and talents, which only you possess, are valuable? Do you believe that financial independence is possible? Do you believe your future is brighter than your past? Do you believe you control your future? Do you believe that God is for you or against you? Do you believe you deserve success financially, in relationships, and in life in general?

One of my biggest struggles when my finances melted down was forgiving myself for putting my family in a dire financial situation. For years, I felt like I didn't deserve to bounce back because I had been so reckless. I began to believe that I deserved to suffer for my actions. I felt I somehow deserved to have bad health. I wondered why and how my wife could still love me. I was my own worst enemy as I continually tore myself down with my negative thoughts.

Imagine someone daily telling your child or family members that they are stupid. Imagine your child or family members hearing from someone constantly that they deserved to suffer because of their mistakes. Imagine them telling your child or family members that they were unworthy of success. I don't know how most people would react, but I would react swiftly and with whatever means necessary to make it stop. However, many of us talk this way to ourselves daily.

I remember sitting in my office one day having my usual pity party. I was as close to depression as I have ever been. The beach house we owned was at the beginning of the foreclosure process. That meant the mortgage company published, in the legal section of my small-town weekly newspaper, a notice of foreclosure. There, in black and white for everyone to see, were my and my wife's names in the foreclosure notice. There was no hiding our struggle anymore. I remember people whom I assumed saw the notice speaking differently to me. I even had a sweet lady come by my office and bring me a cake. She never mentioned the foreclosure notice, but when she hugged me, she said, "You were just heavy on my mind." I knew she had seen it.

I felt so ashamed. The voice in my head was telling me I deserved the shame. I remember sitting in my office and feeling so down that it was hard to breathe. Every time my phone rang, I would cringe at the thought of another bill collector leaving a nasty voicemail. I didn't want to show my face in public, so I became almost hermit-like. This only added to my loneliness and depressed me even more. For a while, I felt like this nightmare would never end.

This happened after my health scare and was in the beginning of my effort to flood my thoughts with positivity. It took a while to flush all the negativity out of my head. Looking back, I realize that the inspirational and motivational books and CDs I was consuming were the seeds to my breakthrough. My breakthrough came one day when I heard Les Brown (author and motivational speaker) say, "Your struggle did not come to stay; it came to pass." This one sentence triggered something deep inside me.

All of a sudden I began to realize that this would pass. I began to see that somehow I would get through this difficult time. Something happened, and I began to forgive myself for my past actions. I heard Oprah Winfrey (talk-show host and author) say one time, "Forgiveness is giving up hope that your past could have been any different." I began to realize again that there was nothing I could do to change my past, but I completely controlled my future. Once I finally forgave myself, my beliefs began to change. Once my beliefs began to change, my life and circumstances began to change.

Forgiving myself didn't happen in a moment. It was and is an ongoing process. However, forgiveness is the process of removing anger, bitterness, and disappointment. This clearing out of negative emotions opens space for thankfulness, hope, and belief. Once I began the process of letting go of my disappointment, I began to think long term rather than short term. I began to believe in possibility again. I began to visualize myself and my family five to ten years down the road.

I reminded myself that we live in a country where anything is possible. Do you realize that if you set your mind to it, even if you don't have a high school diploma, you could be a doctor in less than ten years? Would it be hard? Of course it would be. Would there be challenges? Of course there would be. Would you have to change your lifestyle and mindset to make it happen? There is no doubt that you would. But if it was your dream and you set your mind to do it or die, the only thing that could keep you from achieving it is you and your willingness to believe it to be possible.

What is your dream? Do you believe it is possible? Has there ever been anyone in history who accomplished your dream? If you are struggling with believing that your dream is possible, study the lives of those who have done or are doing what you want to do. Belief comes from a shift in thinking that something is possible to knowing that it is possible. The more people you meet, study, or spend time with who have achieved your dream or desired life, the more you will begin to believe it is possible for you. You cannot deny the fact that others have achieved your desired life. The question is: do you believe you can and that you deserve your dream or desired life? When you believe it is possible for you, at that moment everything will change. You will be willing to work extra hard; you will be willing to sacrifice things others will not sacrifice. You will push through adversity. You will not accept mediocrity. You will become completely focused on reaching your dream life.

Once you believe something is possible, you take steps to make it come true for you. Imagine a tight rope extended from the roof of one skyscraper to the roof of the next skyscraper. Imagine that two men are going to attempt to walk across the tightrope.

The first man was chosen from the crowd gathering on the street below. He spent the past few months getting up when his alarm clock went off. He drank three cups of coffee, smoked four cigarettes, and read the newspaper before he rushed to his job that morning. All day he kept playing back in his mind the horrible stories he read in the newspaper about murder, scandal, crime, and politics. On his way home, he hit the drive-thru at a fast food restaurant where he picked up a half-pound bacon cheeseburger with large French fries and a thirty-two-ounce Coke. When he got home, he parked on the couch, where he stayed up half the night drinking beer, smoking cigarettes, and watching reality TV shows, crime shows, and gossip news shows. He finally fell asleep at midnight and got five and a half hours of sleep.

He has never seen anybody walk on a tightrope before. Because he has not seen anyone walk a tightrope before, he is not sure if it is possible. When he steps up to the rope, the first thing he does is look down. Fear grips him, and he freezes.

The second man has a different daily routine. He wakes up early and spends time focusing on what he is thankful for in his life. He heads to the gym. He works on building his strength and balance. He comes home, eats a healthy breakfast, and heads off to his job. On the way to work, he listens to a motivational CD that discusses possibility. All day he thinks back on the things he is thankful for and the possibility CD. After work, he practices balancing on a tightrope five feet off the ground in his backyard. He eats a healthy dinner and gets to bed in time for eight hours of sleep.

The second man has studied other people who have walked across high-rise tightropes. He has seen it done by dozens of others. He knows it is possible because he has seen it done. He studied how the others did it. He has been practicing exactly what the other successful tightrope walkers did for months. When he gets up on the tightrope, he finds a focus point where he is headed. No matter what distractions may come, he will not take his eyes or his focus off where he is headed.

I think we all know how this more than likely ends. Although this is hypothetical, we spend a lot of our lives living the way the first guy did, just letting things happen around us instead of making things happen. We are distracted by everything around us because we aren't focused on where we are headed. When I began to believe in my possibility again, I finally realized that there was a better way. I realized that in order for things to change, it was up to me to change. I began to believe that I could change because I spent time with people who had already come out of difficult situations like the one I was battling.

In my heart of hearts, I knew that if I wanted to get better financially then I needed to spend time with people who had done and were doing better than me financially. There is an ancient saying that says when the student is ready, the teacher appears. This was true in my case. I knew a man who had been through some difficult times financially, but he had bounced back. I swallowed my pride one day and told him my situation. I was transparent with him, and he agreed to have lunch with me every so often to see if he could help. His suggestions and support during phone calls and lunches over the next couple of years really made a difference. If you don't know someone personally, find an author or trainer who has been through what you are going through and study them.

As much as this good friend's supportive words meant, the mere fact that I was spending time with someone who had done what I wanted to do proved to me that it could be done. It made me realize that bouncing back was possible because I saw it with my own eyes. For some reason, our bodies struggle to accomplish any more than we see done or believe can be done. Our minds have so much potential that is limited by our thoughts. I saw Tony Robbins (life coach, self-help author, and motivational speaker) do an exercise one time that solidified my thought on our minds' potential.

In order for this to sink in, you have to do this, so no excuses. Stand up, raise your right arm in front of you, and point straight ahead with your pointing finger. Keep your legs straight and rotate your fully extended arm with the finger pointing to the right around your body. Once you rotate around, notice where you are pointing. Then rotate back to where you began. Relax with your arm down. Now raise your right arm with your finger pointing straight ahead again. This time do not actually rotate your arm but close your eyes and visualize rotating your arm twice as far as you did before then rotate visually back to straight ahead. One more time with your eyes closed, visualize rotating your arm three times as far around your body. Open your eyes and straighten your arm out with your finger pointing straight ahead. Again, rotate your arm around and notice how much further you are able to rotate just by visualizing that it could be done.

If you haven't done it yet, do it now because this is a powerfully visual point that I want to sink in to your long-term memory.

Can you believe that with just a few seconds of visualization, your mind could add that much flexibility? The amazing part of this is when you grasp that this is just ten to fifteen seconds of visualization and thoughts in your mind that created 10 to 20 percent improvement in flexibility. Now imagine the impact daily of filling your mind with possibilities instead of limiting beliefs. This is why motivational CDs and biographies of people who have overcome obstacles are so important to feed your mind. This is why you should watch YouTube videos on inspiration and motivation daily. This is why sowing positive thinking seeds is so important if you desire to reap more than you are reaping now.

Roger Bannister, in 1954, was the first man to run a mile in less than four minutes. People had been running races for hundreds and thousands of years, and no one had ever run a mile in under four minutes until Bannister. It was widely believed that the human body was not capable of running a sub-four-minute mile. Because it was believed to be physically impossible, it had never been done.

Roger Bannister believed it was possible. Once Bannister broke the four-minute mile, there were over twenty additional people who broke the four-minute-mile barrier over the next six years. Now four-minute miles are routine, and even some high school runners routinely run miles in less than four minutes. Once Roger Bannister proved it could be done, others believed it was possible. Whatever your dream might be, it is possible. You just simply need to study those who have achieved your dream and begin to believe.

One of the most famous sentences in the English language comes from The Declaration of Independence. It is the second sentence and sets the stage for one of the most historically significant documents of all time: "We hold these truths to be self-evident." The founding fathers started off The Declaration of Independence by stating what they believed and what they were willing to die to see come forth. In mathematics, a self-evident truth is defined as a universally accepted principle that requires no proof.

What truths in your life do you hold to be self-evident? What are you willing to sacrifice in order to see your beliefs come to pass? Who will suffer if you do not pursue and achieve the dream that was in you from birth? You must believe that you deserve more than mediocrity. You must believe in possibility. Every person and everything God creates is built to multiply. People, fruit trees, ideas, movements, and, yes, your dreams are all made to multiply. I love what Deion Sanders (former NFL and MLB player) said in his Pro Football Hall of Fame induction speech: "If your dream ain't bigger than you, there's a problem with your dream."

Understand and believe that your dream isn't just about you. It is about the others that it will affect. It is about the ripple effect it will have in your family for generations to come. Believe and understand that you have to move forward. You can't stay where you are because where you are is not where you are supposed to end up. Let hope incubate into belief. Hebrews 11:1 says, "Now faith is the assurance of things hoped for, the conviction of things not seen." Believe in your dream. Believe in things not seen. Believe in yourself.

QUESTIONS TO ASK YOURSELF:

1. **What do I believe in?**

2. **Do I believe my future can be better than my past?**

3. **Am I doing anything to make sure my future is better than my past, or am I just hoping?**

4. **What is my dream for my life?**

5. **Has anyone else accomplished what I want to accomplish?**

ACTION STEPS:

1. Make a list of ten people you know or know of who have come back from your current setback. Become a student of what they did to bounce back.

2. Read or listen to an audio book that is about someone who has succeeded in the area of your dream. To find one, all you have to do is Google the phrase "book about _____."

3. Visualize your dream life in the future. Be specific. What will your average day involve? Where will you live? What will your family look like? Who will your friends be or what will they be like? What will financial freedom look like to you? What groups or organizations will you support financially and with your talents? This will put your subconscious mind to work on preparing the way.

4. Fill in the blank of the following sentence and write it out fifty times a day for ten days in a row: I forgive myself for _____. Writing things out moves them to long-term memory. Writing it out five hundred times is just over seven times seventy, which has significance.

5. Write out your own personal declaration of independence. Write out ten truths that you hold to be self-evident. Pin it up somewhere so you can see it daily.

Chapter 6

Step 4: Find a Mentor or Coach

How to Gain Wisdom and Vision through Accountability

"Two are better than one because they have a good return for their labor: If either of them falls down, one can help the other up. But pity anyone who falls and has no one to help them up."

Ecclesiastes 4:9-10

We are born with a desire deep inside us to reach higher and to do more. In order for us to learn something new, at some point someone has to teach us in order for us to grow. We may learn from a book, but ultimately we learned from the author instead of the book. There has never been a single person who has walked the face of this earth who is completely self-made. Everyone who reaches above average in any area of his or her life has someone to thank for that success.

The process of growth and learning begins with how we are taught from a young age. A child is taught manners, etiquette, and general life skills by a parent or guardian. Children enter kindergarten with a set of specific skills they need to master in order to be able to move on to first grade. He or she is led through this growth by his or her teachers as well as parents or guardians. This continues in the educational system each year until high school graduation. In Boy Scouts or Girl Scouts, you must accomplish certain skills to earn badges and move up to the next level. This is facilitated by leaders. In high school sports, you must learn to perform certain skills in order to move from junior varsity to varsity. This is led by coaches. As youths, we are surrounded by parents, teachers, coaches, and others who guide us into adulthood.

The problem is that once we reach adulthood, many of us stop having others who give us a plan of action to move forward, like teachers or coaches. This leads to wandering through life without direction. Every single time I have achieved success in my life, I had someone coaching me, mentoring me, holding me accountable, or guiding me. Every time I have suffered failures or setbacks, I have been flying solo.

Think about how wars are won. The first thing the enemy attempts to do in a war is to cut off communication. If the soldier on the battlefield does not have anyone else directing him, he will make decisions in the heat of the battle that may not be wise. It isn't because he wants to make a bad decision; he just doesn't have all the facts and doesn't have the ability to see everything going on around him. He depends on information from others who can see the entire battlefield. He depends on those who have a better view of when the proper time to attack or retreat might be. He is always more effective when he has guidance from others who can see the entire battlefield.

How much easier is it to see the mistakes other people are making in their lives than it is to see them in our own lives? Why is it that once we reach adulthood our pride tells us we can handle things on our own? Remember when I mentioned in a previous chapter how alone I felt in the MRI room? I had isolated myself from others so much that, in a way, I was alone.

Think back on your life and the times when things were going your way. Think of achievements you have accomplished. I would imagine there was someone who helped you reach that achievement. Maybe it was your parents or a guardian, maybe a teacher who believed in you or a coach's words of encouragement. Or maybe a mentor or a true friend gave you sound advice at a critical time in your life. Yes, you might have put the work in, and it was your blood, sweat, and tears that led to an achievement, but without inspiration and guidance from someone, odds are you would not have reached as high as you did.

I want to give you a few examples of how teachers, coaches, and mentors have assisted me in reaching levels I would never have reached on my own. As you read this, think back on the people who have assisted you in your life.

My high school golf coach, Stan Bosenberg, held me accountable that I would be at practice during certain times. He helped me to stay focused on my goal of playing college golf. He took me on visits to universities and introduced me to college coaches. His guidance helped me to achieve my goal of receiving a college scholarship to play golf. I put in the effort, but he kept me focused and moving in a certain direction.

My college golf coach held me even more accountable to perform athletically and academically. He taught me the metaphors between life and golf. He set out goals for me and gave me the daily activities to reach my goals. To this day, I reflect on the life lessons that Dr. Terry Hopper taught me. I did the work when he wasn't around a lot of the time, but Coach Hopper helped me stay focused and develop a plan of action to reach my goals not only on the golf course but in life.

When I left college, I went to work with Merrill Lynch as a stock broker. I was hired into a program where I was assigned a mentor broker. Ray McGovern taught me hard work, and his expectations led me to production levels I would not have achieved without his guidance. His expectation of extra effort and accountability pushed me to work harder than I would have done otherwise.

When I left Merrill Lynch to become a part of my family's real estate business, my mom was the broker. She and my stepfather had my brother and me doing yearly goals since we were teenagers. Because of her, goals were a big part of my real estate career. I also always searched for training programs that would push me to do more than I would do otherwise. ERA, which was the franchise that our family's real estate company was associated with during this time, had a program called "Top Gun." There was no magic to the program; they simply set out a plan and action steps. Each week, we had to report back to the instructor our results on the assignments for the week. They trained us in how to be more effective, but because of the accountability during this program, my results and effectiveness went through the roof.

When I first started asking the questions at the bank, many successful people gave me insight. However, Larry Becker challenged me to find a real estate project that he could do. Larry widened my vision of what was possible for me. He called me out when I talked about doing something instead of doing it. He pushed me to stretch myself.

During my highest income years in real estate development and sales, I hired a business coach for myself and all of the real estate agents in my real estate company. Mike Ullery gave guidance and vision that helped me see things in a way I might have missed. He taught my agents how to manage their time and to set goals that were measurable.

When I started the Gold Party Group LLC, Bob Chavis trained me in how to identify jewelry and to run a gold party company. After I started my company, he and my dad were sounding boards for ideas I had on growing the business. Today, we discuss trends we are seeing and bounce ideas off each other every couple of weeks. Bob and my dad's guidance has been invaluable in my company's success.

Nine months before beginning to write this book, I hired Jimmy Sharpe to spend some time with me and assist me in vision casting. Coach Sharpe is a former player and coach at The University of Alabama under Paul "Bear" Bryant and was also the head coach at Virginia Tech University. We met in a men's Bible study group I attend weekly. I hired him to be a life coach for me. Many of the items we discussed led me to the realization that I had to write this book because it was burning inside me to come out.

With that in mind, I hired Ann McIndoo (author's coach) to assist me in writing my book. Ann's guidance and system has cut months and maybe years off the process of writing this book. She and her staff have given me deadlines to move from one part of the process to the next. That accountability has been immeasurable.

Reflect on your life and your accomplishments. I will guarantee you there was someone who motivated you and guided you to new heights. Knowing this, why as adults do we attempt to go through life in many areas alone? Is it our pride that keeps us from admitting we need help? Is it our pride that makes us fake our way through life?

I heard Kirk Franklin (gospel musician, choir director, and author) say, "You can't get healthy unless you tell the doctor where it hurts." I will go one step further. In life, you can't get healthy if you don't have a doctor. Do you have someone whom you can be perfectly honest with about something you are struggling with and know that he or she will give you sound advice? Do you have a person or group that holds you accountable? Do you have a mentor, or are you mentoring someone?

The reason most of us stall in life as adults is because unlike when we were youths, most of us don't have teachers, coaches, or mentors guiding us. We don't have people encouraging us and keeping us focused on moving forward. We don't have people holding us accountable. The bottom line is that in order for you to get to a higher level in life, whether that be financially, physically, mentally, or spiritually, you must search for trusted accountability and assistance. The year and a half I spent spinning my wheels at the bank, I had no real guidance. I was trying to figure it out on my own.

Six months before my financial meltdown began, Mike Ullery (my business and life coach at the time) told me he didn't think there was anything else he could do for me as a business coach. To be perfectly frank, at that time I felt the same way. My pride had numbed me to my need for guidance. I truly believed it was all because of my actions and my talents that I was having the financial success.

Shortly after Mike and I ended our coaching arrangement, I made back-to-back bad investments. I began to press in order to make up for those mistakes and compounded them with others. I was distant from my wife at that time because I didn't want her to worry. This was when my body just physically shut my voice down from the stress, bad habits, and generally unhealthy living. I have often wondered if I would have continued to make one bad mistake after another if I had kept Mike on as my business coach, and would he not have seen some things that I couldn't see due to the "fog of war"?

I don't know if he would have stopped my meltdown, but I do believe that it could only have helped to have someone who would at least point out areas I should reevaluate. I didn't really have anybody around me at that time whom I confided in and felt comfortable about asking their opinion. When we make decisions on our own, we only base our decisions on our views of the situation. One person's view of a situation is never the full picture.

My wife is one of the wisest women I know. She has an intuition that is far beyond mine when it comes to seeing issues before they blow up. My wife has given me wise counsel many times, and I would have avoided many mistakes had I listened to her. Please do not discount the value of your spouse's feedback, but you need others who aren't as close guiding you as well. We need the view of the battlefield from someone who isn't in the same foxhole.

For instance, my wife has a friend who shares very similar life views and values. They both have three children who are basically the same age. They can be as real as they want to be with each other without worrying about being judged. When they aren't sure how to handle a situation with one of their children, they simply pick up the phone to see what the other person thinks. This helps them make better decisions. It gives them confidence in their decisions and ultimately pushes them both to be better parents. Her counsel to my wife in the area of being a mother is far superior to the counsel that I would give my wife.

Think of life like climbing a mountain. Both life and mountain climbing can be physically demanding and at times dangerous. In order to reach the peak, it takes courage and focus. The most effective way to climb a mountain is in tandem with another person. If there are two people climbing the mountain then they can warn each other if they get to a place where the rocks are slippery or loose. Each time one of them climbs a little higher, they drive a stake into the rock of the mountain. By tying off to the mountain, when (not if) one of them slips, they will only fall a short distance before they are caught by the stake in the mountain and the weight of the other person.

If one of them gets tired or sore then the other person can evaluate whether that individual really needs to rest or just needs to be motivated to push through the temporary pain. If one sees an obstacle that he or she isn't sure he or she can overcome, the other person can, through belief and encouragement, motivate the partner to keep moving forward and reach the new height. Not only do they help each other reach the peak, but they celebrate together the achievements along the way.

You were made to be inspired and to inspire others. You were made to be helped and to help others. You were made to reach the top of the mountain. Although there are valleys in life, you were not created to stay in the valleys. Find a coach, mentor, friend, or teacher to help you get where you are designed to be. Even the Lone Ranger had Tonto.

QUESTIONS TO ASK YOURSELF:

1. **Was there someone in my past who helped me reach an achievement?**

2. **Is there someone in my present who is going to help me reach new heights?**

3. **Do I have someone in my life whom I can bounce ideas off and whose guidance I trust?**

4. **Do I think it is important to have a coach or mentor?**

5. **Who is around me from whom I could learn something to help my dream become a reality?**

ACTION STEPS:

1. Make a list of things you need to learn how to do to move to your next level. Then make a list of people you know who have that skill. Tell them you notice that they are good at _____, and you would like to know how to do _____. Simply ask them if they would take some time and show you how to _____.

2. Find a small group, whether it be through a church or business organization, that has accountability groups.

3. Google how to _____ (whatever it is you are trying to accomplish). Then find blogs and communities where you can learn from others. Post questions, and you will get options that could help move you to the next level.

4. Remember the people in your past who mentored you or taught you. One of them may be the person you need right now to help guide you to your next level in life. If so, start with thanking them for what they did in the past and ask them if they could assist you again.

5. Hire a business or life coach. This is an investment, not an expense.

Chapter 7

Step 5: Set the Course of Your Life with Goals

How to Create a Step-by-Step Guide to Your Dreams

"People with goals succeed because they know where
they are going… It's as simple as that."

Earl Nightingale

Clear-cut goals give you a target in life to work toward. If you never have a destination in mind, how will you know if you get there? I love the quote from Les Brown that says, "Shoot for the moon. Even if you miss, you'll end up among the stars."

I first learned about goals years ago from my mom and stepfather as a teenager. I have been using them effectively my entire life. I have since studied the value and use of goals extensively. I can't tell you how or why writing goals down works, but it does. Physically writing down goals puts your subconscious mind to work to make them happen. All of a sudden it seems like everything around you is conspiring to make your goal a reality for you.

Have you ever bought a new automobile and then suddenly you start seeing the exact same make, model, and color everywhere you go? These vehicles were always there, but now they are a part of your consciousness. Goals are the same way. Once you put them in writing, they become a part of your consciousness. All of a sudden, you begin to see things you didn't notice before. People who have what you need to reach your goals are suddenly all around you. Resources you need to reach your goal suddenly appear. It seems magical. Goals simply bring your desires to your consciousness and open your eyes to what has been there all along.

Goals are targets for our life. Zig Ziglar told a similar story to the one I am about to share with you. I have updated his story, using a personal friend of mine as the example.

One of my best friends is currently a member of the US Army Special Forces. He is the former team sergeant of an elite group of twelve soldiers, the best of the best. He has served seven tours in Iraq and Afghanistan. He is one of the most highly-trained and combat-experienced men on the planet. He has fired, in training and combat, hundreds of thousands of rounds of ammunition. To say that he is good with a rifle would be an understatement. However, I have no doubt in my mind that I could outperform him at target shooting, despite my limited practice, with a couple of conditions. I can do this as long as you allow me to blindfold him and spin him around so that he cannot see or even have any idea of the direction of the target.

Do you see the value of being able to see the target? Have you ever wondered why some people who appear to have less talent than you, maybe less education than you, and are just kind of jerks succeed? Many times it is because they have goals that they focus on achieving on a daily basis. Is there anything more frustrating than having somebody who is basically an idiot and a jerk being more successful than you? Well, the curtain has been pulled back now for you to see why this is so in many cases.

Goals are the target that we all need to stay focused on in order to reach the next level in life. In a previous chapter, I mentioned the man on the tightrope picking out a focal point and keeping his eye focused on moving toward that point. Focusing on exactly where you are headed gives you the ability to avoid constantly noticing the distractions around you. It also fulfills something deep inside us that is built for achievement.

Written goals are like our shopping list for life. Imagine going to the grocery store without a list. As you aimlessly wander through the grocery store, do you think you might spend more money than you intended to spend? Do you think the marketing in the store might be aimed at getting you to buy something that really doesn't serve a purpose in your life? Do you think you might get home after the shopping trip and realize that you forgot something you really needed?

Goals mean different things to different people. Basically, they are something in the future that we would like to achieve, have, or become. In order for them to be effective, they must be specific, measurable, and have a time of completion. They must also be broken down into actionable steps to reach.

Two of the biggest stumbling blocks to achievement of goals are, number one, becoming overwhelmed by everything that needs to be accomplished to reach a goal and, number two, waiting for the perfect opportunity to start. First let me speak about being overwhelmed. Christmas Eve should be one of the most joyous nights of the year, but for me it was a nightmare for years. You see, I am the guy who hates assembling anything. By the time the kids went to bed, my personal hell began every year on Christmas Eve. Boxes and boxes of toys needed assembly for my three kids.

A couple years ago, my dread didn't go away, but things began to get better. The big change? A novel idea of following the directions for assembly. I hated the directions for years. They made me feel incompetent. However, I realized I could assemble almost anything as long as I kept it simple and followed the step-by-step instructions. Don't judge me; you or someone in your family will drive around lost for hours and refuse to stop and ask directions.

Looking at the box containing a trampoline with ninety-seven parts and three hundred-plus screws and bolts can be overwhelming. However, following step one and achieving it then step two and achieving it, etc. makes it doable. Simplicity brings clarity, and clarity brings action. The bigger your dream or goal, the more basic you need the steps to be.

Keep it basic. A goal for many people is to lose weight. Many times diets can be confusing and overwhelming. They can involve not eating this or that. Drinks to avoid and drinks to consume. Where to eat and not to eat. When to eat and when not to eat. By the time you get a few days in, you are so confused and frustrated that you just quit.

For years my weight yo-yoed up and down. I tried the no-carb diet and lost weight. I had measured meal plans delivered to my home and lost weight. I even did the liquid diets for a few days and lost weight. But I always gained it back.

However, things changed for me when I brought it to a basic level. Finally, I realized that in order to lose weight and keep it off, all I had to do was burn more calories per day than I consumed. This meant I needed to eat healthier, but I could eat almost anything within reason as long as I consumed fewer calories per day than I burned. With the advancements today of apps and free website tools, it is easy to keep up with your calorie intake. I used MyFitnessPal, which told me how many calories I could consume and reach my target weight. It also told me how many calories everything I ate contained.

MyFitnessPal also links with Endomondo, which I use. Endomondo is an app that measures how many calories I burned working out. Because they linked together, the calories I burned working out were automatically and instantaneously calculated on Endomondo then they were added automatically to the calories I could consume on MyFitnessPal. Since the app was on my phone, I entered every item that I was going to eat into MyFitnessPal before I ate it. By pausing to enter the food in my diary on MyFitnessPal, it kept me from eating anything without first thinking about it. At the end of the day, the app allowed me to press a button to complete my day. It then calculated what my weight would be in five weeks if I ate and or exercised like that each day for the next five weeks.

MyFitnessPal and Endomondo also have friends sections and newsfeeds. The newsfeed section on Endomondo gives me inspiration. Seeing my friends working out or knowing my friends are seeing if I work out gives me accountability. It helps me push through and work out even when I really don't want to exercise. As a matter of fact, if you join Endomondo, friend me. With the readers of this book friending me, it will motivate me even more to stay focused on my health goals and will hopefully help you as well.

While I am on the topic of diet and exercise, I have to share with you that it is quite ironic that I am sharing tips on healthy living. I guess this is like the former alcoholic assisting the alcoholic. After all, I am only a few years removed from being thirty-plus pounds overweight, binge eating, and chain smoking. From that standpoint, understand that if I can do it...well, you know the rest.

The second reason we fail to get started with goals and have achievements is that we get distracted by thinking everything has to be perfect before we can start. The desire for the perfect circumstances can lead to a "failure to launch."

A basketball coach once told me that you make exactly zero percent of the shots you don't take. Waiting for the perfect circumstances is really nothing more than living a life where you just let things happen instead of making them happen. Success in life will never just happen.

Imagine a large military artillery unit waiting until it feels it has the perfect coordinates and wind conditions to fire its weapons. It will end up being destroyed before it ever fires a shot. Instead, they make their best estimation and fire. If the first shot misses, they make adjustments based on where it landed and fire again. It may take one shot or it may take many shots, but sooner or later they are going to hit their target. Fire your weapon! Make adjustments if need be but don't wait for the perfect timing because it will never exist.

Explaining how to effectively set goals is extensive, and there have been many complete books written on the subject. For the sake of time, I want to give you some easy, quick action steps that you can apply immediately. If you would like more detailed training on goals, visit my website at www.domorehavemorebe-more.com and look for the goals video after clicking on the video tab. In that video, I will walk you through an easy-to-follow goal-setting program.

The first step is to list your immediate needs and your desires. For instance, if you need to get out of credit card debt then that needs to be listed. If you want to, for instance, become a real estate agent then put it on your list. The second step is to put a timeframe on when you want to achieve it. The third step is to break it down into monthly, weekly, and daily activities.

Let's take getting out of credit card debt as an example. Let's say you have balances of six thousand dollars in credit card debt, and you want to have it paid off in two years. The first step is to obviously stop using the card and growing the balance owed. The second step is to divide your six-thousand-dollar debt by twenty-four months. That comes to $250 per month that you need to pay your cards down on top of your monthly minimum interest payments. If we divide $250 by thirty (rounded-off number of days in a month) then we see that you need to find a way to either (or both) cut out of your current spending or add an income of $8.33 per day that you can apply to your credit card balances in order to be rid of your credit card debt in two years.

Put these items in writing. Then develop a plan for how you will get that extra $250 per month, and write it down. It might say, "I will have a yard sale to generate a portion of the $250 this month. I will cut out my Starbucks coffee two days a week to generate a portion of the $250 this month. I will take on an additional part-time job to generate the $250 per month." Whatever it is, formulate a written plan of action and do it.

Now let's take the goal of becoming a real estate agent. The first step is to find out the minimum requirements to receive a real estate license. The second step is to find out what other skills you can learn that will increase the likelihood of your success as a real estate agent. If you know that you need to attend a class and pass a state exam in order to become licensed then write them on your list. If you learn that the ability to find home sellers or buyers will help, add that to your list. Then set a date when you will achieve this goal.

Create an action plan that says, "I will enroll in the state-required real estate course by [a certain date]. I will complete the real estate course by [a certain date] and schedule my state exam by [another date]. During month one, on top of attending my class, I will find materials and training to study on locating home sellers and buyers. In month two, I will find materials or training to study on locating home buyers." You get the picture. Create an action plan and work the plan.

Written, specific, measurable goals with deadlines have played a huge part in any successes I have seen in my life, whether they were mental, physical, spiritual, financial, or relational. During the times in my life that I have suffered setbacks or losses, almost all were during periods when I lacked clear goals and a vision of where I wanted to go or be in the future. This one step can change the trajectory of your life.

Commit to your future. Stop reacting to life and start making life react to you. Take control of your life. If you are in a struggle now, you must realize that you are the only one who can get you out of this struggle. If you want to get better results, formulate a plan of action and get to work.

On average, we are only given roughly 27,375 days on this earth. Don't delay; every single day is important. Take your shot. Fire your weapon. Even if you fail, it is better than looking back on a life filled with "should haves" or "could haves." You are designed to move forward. Do what you need to do and were designed to do now. Do it for yourself, your family, your God. Many times the process of reaching a goal is even more fulfilling than achieving it. Set your course and sail into your destiny.

QUESTIONS TO ASK YOURSELF:

1. If I keep doing what I am doing now, will my life be better or worse one year, five years, or ten years from now?

2. Do I have written goals for my life?

3. Are my goals specific, measurable, attainable, and set to a time-table for achievement?

4. Am I doing things daily to move my life in a positive direction?

5. Am I reacting to life, or is life reacting to me?

ACTION STEPS:

1. Go to my website at www.domorehavemorebemore.com and let me walk you through the free training on setting your goals. This video will give you an action plan that is clear, concise, and attainable for you to reach your goals.

2. Make a to-do list each night before you go to bed of your items to achieve the next day. This one step will give you the ability to wake up in action mode instead of reaction mode.

3. Read your written goals daily to keep them in focus and a part of your consciousness.

4. Read or listen to a book every month on your future dream job. If you read or listen to a book a month, by the end of the year you will have knowledge superior to most people who are already doing your dream job. Knowledge is power.

5. Draw out a chart for measurable goals. If your goal is to lose twenty pounds then draw a barometer that has the numbers one through twenty going up the barometer. Put this barometer on the mirror in your bathroom. Every time you weigh in and have lost a pound, fill in the barometer to the amount you have lost. This also works for savings goals and getting out of debt goals.

Chapter 8

Step 6: Change Your Way to Greatness
How to Make Changes That Transform Your Life

"It may be hard for an egg to turn into a bird: it would be a jolly sight harder for it to learn to fly while remaining an egg. We are like eggs at present. And you cannot go on indefinitely being just an ordinary, decent egg. We must be hatched or go bad."

C.S. Lewis

Wherever you are right now, spiritually, physically, financially, mentally, or relationally, you were not meant to stay there. You were made to move to the next level. There is no such thing as maintaining. You are either getting better or you are getting worse. In order to reach the next level in life, change must occur. Although each chapter has discussed change, I want to emphasize a few areas that you must focus on to move to your next level.

When most people hear the word "change," it makes them uncomfortable. People who think of change in a negative way are almost always reacting to their lives instead of creating their lives. No matter how much you hate change, change is one of the few things that you can be rest assured is going to happen. The question becomes whether you will create positive changes in your life or you will react to the negative changes that will always come if you don't take charge.

In order for you to reach a desired level of achievement in any area of your life, you have to first change yourself. You must become a student of whatever it is that you want to become. Read books on it. Watch videos on it. Immerse yourself in the knowledge, skills, and attributes you need to possess in order to become what it is that you desire to become. You must transform yourself into what it is you desire and were created to become.

If you want to get a raise or promotion at your current job, become the person and develop the skills that deserve the raise or promotion. The raise or promotion will surely come. If you desire to be debt free, learn the skills and have the discipline to become a person that is debt free. If you desire more friends, become a person who people want to call their friend. Sometimes we have to become the person we want others around us to be in order for them to change as well. If you want your kids to be kind to others, be kind to others. If you want your coworkers to be more positive, be more positive. If you want a spouse who is less self-focused, be less self-focused.

In a previous chapter, I discussed quitting smoking during my illness. Can we all agree that bad habits are extremely hard to break, and until we get a big enough "why" for stopping something, we can relapse? Well, I was guilty of relapse. Once I got my voice back and the struggles were still present, I had a relapse. I began smoking again, and my weight was more out of control than it had ever been. My daughters were older now, and we had added a son to our family. I attempted to hide it from my kids. Did I really think they couldn't smell it on me?

My wife began running and working out during this time. She began to get in great shape; physically, she was in as good a shape as she was when we got married and before having our three kids. One day, she came in from running, and I said, "I have to tell you that you look good. I really appreciate how hard you are working to look so good." It was as if she had been planning this for months. She then said, "Jimmy, you're a good husband. You deserve a wife that takes care of herself." My pride swelled that she cared so much about me that she was doing it for me. As I walked outside to smoke, I caught a glimpse of my rotund, unhealthy profile in the mirror. I said to myself, *I can't believe it; she got me.* The next day I bought running shoes.

What she realized was that if she wanted me to be healthier then she had to get so healthy that I wanted to join her. It worked. However, the influence others around us have works both ways. Think back to when you were a teenager. Do you remember how strong peer pressure was on you? If all your friends were taking part in craziness then you felt pressure to fit in and act crazy as well. This was despite everything inside you screaming that you should not participate.

As we become adults, we think we get over peer pressure. In reality, we just become numb to it. Earlier in the book, we discussed being the average of the five people we spend the most time around. As adults, we don't think of peer pressure, but in reality we are more under the influence of those we spend the majority of time with than we realize. We begin to adjust our actions to those we are around. Do you have a friend who has poor grammar or uses language that you would not normally use? Do you speak differently when you are around him or her than you normally do? This is an example of adjusting to your surroundings.

However, like my wife's positive influence on me, there is such a thing as positive peer pressure. If you want to do more, have more, or be more in any area of your life then spend time with the people who will make you adjust your life in that direction. I once heard Les Brown quote Sir Sydney Poitier (actor and author) from his book *The Measure of a Man,* where Poitier says, "When you go for a walk with someone, something happens without being spoken, either you adjust to their pace or they adjust to your pace." The question becomes: whose pace are you adjusting to on a daily basis? Is their pace making you increase or decrease your pace?

The hardest part of changing myself physically was to quit smoking forever. I had quit before, and I had always started back. My wife came to me one day and said, "Libby [my oldest daughter, who was thirteen years old at the time] asked why Daddy smoked." My wife told me she was really upset. For the first time in my life, my eyes were peeled open to the impact my smoking would have on my kids' lives. I began to realize that my actions could either create or end generational curses.

I had seen my dad smoke all his life, so it wasn't that hard for me to start. My dad had seen his dad smoke all of his life, so it wasn't that hard for him to start. I realized that if I quit smoking, odds were that my kids wouldn't smoke and struggle with what I struggled with throughout my life. I decided to break the generational curse rather than pass it on to my children.

If you have a specific struggle, odds are you saw one or both of your parents struggle with the same issue. If you wonder why you struggle with a certain area (alcoholism, drug addiction, being overweight, bad relationships, lack of commitment, financial struggle, etc.), wonder no more. The scary thing is that if you don't break the trend or share this information with your children or grandchildren then they will more than likely struggle in the same area.

All of a sudden, my "why" for quitting smoking was bigger than just my health. My quitting smoking could affect generations to come. Quitting became bigger than making my wife happy (although that is very important). Quitting became about grandchildren and great-grandchildren that I may never meet. I wanted to leave a generational blessing rather than a generational curse.

I realized that I needed accountability to make this work. I decided to burn all my bridges, where retreat was not an option. Sometimes you need to have no way out in order to fight through the struggle. The first way that I burned my bridges was having a talk with my then-thirteen-year-old daughter. It was emotional, and for the first time in her life, I was transparent with her about my shortcomings. The older I get, the more I believe transparency breeds trust. I told her that I had been attempting to hide my smoking from her because I knew the reason I first started smoking was because I assumed it was okay since my dad smoked.

Then I burned my bridge. I looked her in the eye, and I told her, "I am going to quit, and I will never smoke again. I am telling you this because if I ever smoke again, you will have the ability to question everything I tell you going forward." Once you tell your child something like that, there is no turning back. This helped me get through it and in turn strengthened her belief in me. Be careful in making these kinds of promises to your kids. Make sure you will do what you say or you are willing to die trying if you are going to make a promise like this to someone you love. No matter how hard it got, it was not as hard as losing my daughter's faith in me. When it got hard, I would continually tell myself that pain is temporary, but my daughter's trust was for a lifetime.

I also told the group of twenty or so men in my weekly Bible study that I was quitting smoking. I admired these men and hated admitting my weakness, but I knew they would be supportive, and I knew that some of them would check on me. I knew that the next week I would be asked how it was going, and I could not lie to these men that I respect and admire so much.

I quit cold turkey on September 11, 2011. It sucked! The physical withdrawal pain was horrible. However, every time I didn't think I could get through it, I remembered my "why." I would visualize the effect of my daughter not believing in me. I would visualize having to tell one of the men I respected that I had failed and started back smoking. I visualized my wife's disappointment. I visualized generations to come of healthy grandchildren and great-grandchildren. I made myself focus on long-term effects rather than short-term, temporary pain.

I will never forget the date September 11. Now it is not only a day to remember for tragedy but also for personal triumph—not just triumph for me but for generations to come. If you are struggling with a certain area of your life right now, the way to change right now is to burn your bridges. Make your triumph over it bigger than just being about you. Realize that your success in overcoming your struggle is a pebble in the pond that will have ripples for generations to come. Having a desire to do things for ourselves has power, but doing things for others gives you a whole other level of motivation. The bigger your reason for overcoming a personal struggle, the easier it will be to overcome. Change is never easy, but in order for things to change in your life, it has to start with you.

In previous chapters we discussed a need to change your attitude, beliefs, and the people you spend the most time around. I believe who you spend time with and are around the most plays the most significant role in your ability to change your attitude, beliefs, and ultimately your life. Simply put, you must surround yourself with positive people.

When I was young, my dad lived near Destin, Florida, and he used to take me and some of my friends crabbing on Crab Island (before it became the location it is today as one of the world's largest on-water, sandbar party spots). He would pull the boat to the side of the sandbar, where the tide would drift us across the knee-deep to waist-deep water. He would cut the engine off and tie a rope affixed to an old tin washtub that would float behind the boat as the tide moved the boat. My dad would stand up on the front of the boat and point the crabs out as he saw them moving away from the approaching boat. As soon as he pointed them out, one of us teenage boys would jump off the boat to chase the crab down with a net. Once the crab was caught, we would walk around and empty it into the washtub floating behind the boat. In a relatively short period of time, this usually resulted in a washtub full of crabs to within a few inches of the top.

One day, as we headed home with a washtub full of crabs, I realized we never put a top over the washtub. I wondered why these crabs didn't just crawl out of the washtub to freedom and safety. As I thought about this, I noticed a few crabs that began to crawl to the side to make their apparent easy getaway. Each one of them almost made it out when one of the other crabs would reach up with his pinchers and pull the crab right back into the washtub. The crab that wanted to get out of the mess would literally have to sacrifice the leg the other crab was clinging to in order to escape. Many didn't even attempt to free themselves from the "misery loves company" crab. The "misery loves company" crab would be so determined to keep the other crab from escaping that when we were finished boiling the crabs, many times they died never letting go.

Isn't it amazing how many people in this world are like the crab? Misery truly does love company. While you make a move to get past a situation, the only move they make is to keep you there with them. "Crab-like" people prey on others during times of distress. They surround themselves with others that are of like mind. We all have them around us. You just thought of the ones around you right now. In order for you to reach new heights, you have to remove yourself from the crab-like people.

Although change can be painful, it is necessary. You know the changes you need to make. The key to finally making them is to get your "why" big enough that you are willing to burn all bridges of retreat. Your life purpose is bigger than waking up to an alarm clock, going to work, coming home to watch TV, and going to sleep just so you can do it all over again the next day. Your life purpose will inspire others. It will change the trajectory of your family and friends. Your life purpose is solely yours. The world needs your impact. That burning desire inside you was not placed there to stay inside you. Positive change is not an option; it is a must! We need you to get off the sidelines and into the game. The time is now.

QUESTIONS TO ASK YOURSELF:

1. **Are there things I need to change in my life?**

2. **Do I spend a lot of time with crab-like people?**

3. **Who are the crab-like people around me?**

4. **What generational curse can I end?**

5. **What is my "why"?**

ACTION STEPS:

1. Write out your "why" or "whys" that you must make a change. This could take five minutes or five days. Whatever it takes, just reading it should emotionally move you to action. If it doesn't, keep working on it until it does.

2. Write out your "why" on a three-by-five-inch index card and place it on the dashboard of your car near the speedometer, where you will see it every day.

3. Change the route you drive to work. Change what time you eat lunch. Eat a different lunch than you usually eat. Call an old friend who is positive and catch up. Change as many small things as you can think of in order to get yourself in the change mode.

4. Change your schedule. Go to bed at night one hour earlier. Wake up one hour earlier in the morning. Use this hour to do something physically, spiritually, and mentally enriching. Your whole world will change if you start each day this way. Don't you dare say you're not a morning person. Most high achievers follow the schedule I just mentioned. Crabs sleep in. Which do you want to be, and how bad do you want it?

5. Take a walk with someone you love, especially if you haven't done this in a long time.

Chapter 9

Step 7: Turn Your Mess into Your Message
How to Create Your Enduring Legacy

"The purpose of life is a life of purpose."

Robert Byrne

Something inside you has been lying dormant for years. It's the call of your heart. It's your passion. It's your dream. Maybe your current or past struggle was simply placed in your life to reignite your life's purpose. Sometimes it takes having nothing to lose for you to realize that you have everything to gain. Sometimes the thing we view as the worst thing that could happen to us becomes the greatest and most pivotal moment in elevating us to our dream lives.

Many times our dream lives are like the Chinese bamboo. The Chinese bamboo can take four or more years to break ground after it has been planted. The four- to five-year average time period for it to break ground is based on the seed being properly fertilized and watered regularly. If the seed is neglected then it can take much longer for the tree to break ground, assuming it ever does.

However, once the bamboo breaks ground, it is one of the fastest-growing plants in the world. It can grow to almost one hundred feet tall in a four-month period. It can grow as much as thirty-nine inches in a twenty-four-hour period. It grows so fast that you can almost watch it grow.

Has your dream and purpose been planted or appeared dormant for a while? Have you watered or fertilized it lately? It may only need a little care or attention to break through the ground. It is easy to realize that I can make one stupid mistake and in an instant ruin my marriage, my financial life, or any other area of my life. I believe this principle can be applied for the good as well. I believe you can make one decision, one action, or one change at this moment, and you can unleash tremendous growth in all areas of your life. It may take time to manifest, but it will become when, not if, you will see it.

Sometimes it takes time for your dream to appear, but when it appears it was always worth the struggle and the wait. The farmer who nurtures the Chinese bamboo makes a consistent effort to water and fertilize the seed for years without seeing any signs of growth. However, he believes with all his heart that if he continues to consistently water and fertilize the seed, there will come a day when he will see amazing growth in a short period of time. His patience, faith, and consistency in the end are rewarded. You might not have seen any indication of growth in your life yet, but amazingly fast growth is just around the corner if you will be diligent in preparing for it and caring for it.

I have seen my financial situation change in an instant from lack to surplus. I have seen my health move from sickness to wellness in a very short period of time. I have seen my marriage move from okay to tremendous in a short period of time. I have seen hopeless situations miraculously reversed to victories in the blink of an eye. It is time for your miracle. It is time for your mess to become your message. It is time to cross the line from being a seed to a vibrant, growing, fruit-producing tree.

The world has waited long enough. It is time to give birth to your dream life. It is time to quit making excuses and start making progress. It's time to focus on others instead of yourself. It's time to remember that you cannot change your past, but you can change your future. It is time to be transformed into all you were created to be.

At some point we all start out like caterpillars. The caterpillar just slowly moves and wanders aimlessly through each day. It eats leaves. The plant is created to serve many purposes, one of which is to provide a few leaves for the caterpillar to eat. However, the caterpillar often eats so many leaves that it actually kills the very plant that is providing its nourishment. The caterpillar is a taker. It lives a life in which it slithers from place to place on its belly with seemingly no purpose. But the caterpillar is not made to stay in this state.

There comes a moment when something inside the caterpillar knows that it can no longer be a lowly caterpillar. Its nature, deep inside, tells it that it must change. Although the decision to change can happen in a moment, the process of changing takes time. The caterpillar spins itself into a cocoon or chrysalis, where it cannot be disturbed or distracted by the outside world. Inside this cocoon, it is completely focused on transforming into what it is designed to be and do.

One day the butterfly realizes that it has developed to a point where it must come out of the cocoon. However, the process of coming out of the cocoon is a major struggle. It takes time and effort for the butterfly to come out of the cocoon. This struggle is the final transformation of the butterfly. During the struggle to remove itself from the cocoon, the fluid in the butterfly's body is pushed out from the center of the body and into the wings to complete their development. The bigger the struggle, the more the wings develop. Without the struggle, the wings of the butterfly (the most critical part of its ability to fly) will not develop.

Once the struggle to remove itself from the cocoon is complete, a beautiful butterfly emerges. It soars gracefully through the sky and is admired by everyone who sees it. The butterfly receives its nourishment from nectar that the flowers produce for it. The butterfly does not take from the flower. The flower gladly provides the nectar for the butterfly in return for the butterfly picking up the flower's pollen on its feet and wings. In order for the flower's reproduction cycle to continue, the butterfly carries the pollen to the next flower that provides it with additional nectar. Instead of being a taker like the caterpillar, the butterfly is a partner. Instead of possibly killing the plant that it receives its nourishment from like the caterpillar, the butterfly assists the flowers in bringing forth new life. As a matter of fact, the more flowers the butterfly helps by spreading its pollen, the more it is fed.

We have all experienced the different stages of life like the caterpillar and the butterfly. Realize that you were not created to be a taker like the caterpillar but rather a giver like the butterfly. There is a time for each of us to be transformed from what we are today into what we were designed to become. The cocoon is a place where the caterpillar was safe from the distractions and dangers of the outside world. You may think you have naysayers around you, but can you imagine what the caterpillar heard before he surrounded himself with the protective cocoon? I can just hear the other caterpillars now, "You want to do what? You really think that you can transform yourself from what we are into a butterfly? You think you can fly? You are completely crazy!" Realize that sometimes we have to isolate ourselves from others who don't have the capacity to see the dream inside us.

Please understand that the only way the butterfly doesn't emerge victoriously from the cocoon is if it quits instead of pushing through the struggle no matter how hard it gets. Let me rephrase this for you: the only way you do not become all you were created to be is if you quit. The main reason the sky is not full of butterflies is because many quit when the struggle gets difficult. The main reason the world is not filled with successful people is because most people quit when the struggle gets hard.

The harder your struggle is right now or has been in the past, the more developed your wings will be and the higher you can soar. The butterfly has a completely different view of life as it gracefully soars in the sky than the caterpillar does on its belly on the leaf. It is time for you to get off your belly. It is time to isolate yourself in order to transform yourself. It is time to realize that you cannot quit no matter how hard your struggle is right now. Never forget that if it were easy, the sky would be filled with butterflies, and successful people would be everywhere. You must do what it takes today to have what you want tomorrow.

Ultimately our personal struggles and our lives aren't about us. There are people who are only two steps behind where you are in a similar struggle. They need to hear encouragement from you that they can move forward. Share your story with others. If you have been through a divorce, tell somebody going through it now that they will make it like you did. If someone is struggling with a sickness or disease that you overcame, share your story of triumph with them. If you have suffered financial loss and bounced back, give them a vision of recovery through your story. Your struggle is connected to your purpose!

The world needs you to fulfill your purpose. We need your dreams to become reality, not for you but for the people that it inspire and affect in a positive way. Your legacy will be determined by who you affect in a positive way. Your legacy will endure time if it is based on helping others. I dare you to do something anonymously for someone else that helps them and has no benefit to you. There is no better feeling in the world than helping others along life's path.

Your season of dormancy is over. Stand up and walk into the greatness you were created to achieve. You were born to live a passionate, victorious life not, just for you but as an inspiration to others. There is nothing left but to do what you do and become what you were created to become.

QUESTIONS TO ASK YOURSELF:

1. What dream or purpose in my life has been lying dormant for years?

2. What have I overcome?

3. How can I encourage others with my story of victory?

4. Who would I inspire by living a purposeful life?

ACTION STEPS:

1. Do something anonymous and random to make others smile. Examples include: pay the toll for the car behind you at a tollbooth and tell the attendant to tell them to have a blessed day. Ask a waitress to add a military person's lunch or dinner to your bill and tell the waitress to tell them thank you after you leave. Pay for a pack of Lifesavers in the grocery line and ask the cashier to give it to the mom with kids in the back of the line when she checks out while telling her to cherish the moments with her kids. Be creative but focus on making others smile.

2. Write out a short version of your story of how you have overcome something. Include how you felt in the process, how you overcame the struggle, and how your life is different now because of your struggle. Have it ready and email it to people as you see others that you could encourage. Believe me, it will amaze you how many times this opportunity will come up and how much it will encourage you by encouraging them.

3. Google online forums about whatever you have overcome. You can post your story on the forum anonymously if you are not comfortable sharing it with people you don't know yet. You will still have the ability to get your message out and gain confidence.

4. If you are still in your struggle, Google forums about your struggle, and you will find inspiration to keep moving forward.

Conclusion

The key to achievement is always action. The action steps I offer at the end of each chapter are there to encourage you to get moving because action starts momentum. The first step is always the hardest. Do something! If it doesn't work, do something else! Sooner or later you will figure it out and experience a life-changing breakthrough. Change can happen in the blink of an eye. But it will only happen if you make it happen.

Make sure the person you become five years from now is thankful for the sacrifices you make today instead of being bitter about your lack of action. You were born for more—more joy, more peace, more love, and all that this life has to offer. Create a legacy that has positive ripple effects for generations to come. You control your future. Now go out and be all you were created to be. You have all the tools you need. You can do this. You will do this!

In the words of Dr. Seuss, "Oh, the places you'll go."

Personal Note from Jimmy

My hope is that this book helps you in some way. Since this book is about my life experiences and how I overcame some of my struggles, I want to share with you what has always worked for me and what I believe. I believe that each of us is divinely and perfectly created. We are all gifted with unique characteristics and talents. We are all endowed with a purpose. I believe that the unique talents and purposes we are each individually given have one common thread. In some way, shape, or form, all talents and purposes are designed, at their core, to help others.

I believe, as Pierre Teilhard de Chardin said, "We are not human beings having a spiritual experience. We are spiritual beings having a human experience." Throughout this book, I have discussed the steps to bouncing back from challenges and struggles. I believe you cannot improve God's plan. The core of the seven steps to bouncing back in this book are similar to the steps to restoration and a personal relationship with a Living God. The Christian plan of salvation follows a roadmap type plan to redemption, which includes admitting where we have fallen short, believing in Christ, changing what we have been doing, and turning our mess into our message. It's not about being perfect; it's about being forgiven.

Without my faith, I could not have overcome the obstacles and challenges I have faced. My faith grows with every obstacle that He helps me overcome. I know that God is for me, and I know that He is for you. Although struggles may seem great, and battles may be lost, I cling to the passage from Romans 8:31 that says, "What, then, shall we say in response to these things? If God is for us, who can stand against us?" (NIV)

Whatever you may be facing, realize that you may not be able to see it right now, but God is at work. Romans 8:28 says, "And we know that in all things God works for the good of those who love Him, who have been called according to His purpose." (NIV) I have found through my struggles that even when I could not see any good in my struggle, the key word in this passage is "all." It doesn't say that in "some" things God works for the good; it says in "all" things. Whether you realize it or not, God is at work to turn your current struggle into something good.

My bounce back financially came through a gold party company where we recycled old gold jewelry. I studied the process of the refinement of gold. Although machines do most of the work today, I love the process that was used for thousands of years.

The gold ore was heated by the goldsmith in a process that would melt the metal. The heat would be increased in an effort to burn off all impurities and to make the gold shine as bright as possible. The end goal of the goldsmith was to purify the gold completely. As he would continue to increase the heat, even the most stubborn impurities would eventually be burned away. The goldsmith knew the purity process was complete when the gold became so shiny that he could see his reflection in it.

If you are struggling today, realize that the fire may be hot, but your impurities are melting away. Sometimes the most difficult circumstances result in the greatest victories. God loves you. He wants to give you the peace that can only come from Him. If you have never opened a Bible before, begin in the book of John and just start reading. It will change your life. I know this because it changed mine.

Recommendations

Throughout the pages of this book, I refer to quotes from authors, speakers, teachers, and thought-leaders that I learned from along the way. I want to give honor where it is due so I would like to share additional information about these experts. Where available, I will share the expert's website. However, a sample for most of these experts can be found with a simple search on www.youtube.com. This recommendations page is in the order in which they appear in the book. Remember, seekers find, and the message these experts share is a great place to start seeking.

George Mason was one of the founding fathers of the United States of America.

Jack Canfield is a motivational speaker and author. He is best known as the co-creator of the Chicken Soup for the Soul book series. He also authored the book *The Success Principles* which I found to have great insight. www.jackcanfield.com

Brian Tracy is a motivational speaker and author. He is recognized by many as one of the all-time great speakers and trainers. His *Psychology of Success* program was one of the most impactful programs I ever completed. www.briantracy.com

Zig Ziglar was a motivational speaker and author. He is recognized as one of the most influential personal growth and motivational speakers of all time. His work and specifically his book *Over the Top* has been one of the biggest driving forces behind any successes I have ever achieved. www.ziglar.com

Dr. Maya Angelou is an author and poet. Her writings, quotes and simply the sound of her voice always inspire me. www.mayaangelou.com

Eric Thomas is a motivational speaker and author. He is recognized as the new breed of motivational speaker. His career was launched with weekly 5-10 minute motivational videos on youtube. Everything he does inspires me, including his book *The Secret to Success*. www.etinspires.com

Bob Proctor is motivational speaker and author. The most impactful book I read of his was *You Were Born Rich*. www.bobproctor.com

Theodore Roosevelt Jr. was the 26th President of the United States of America.

Tenth Avenue North is a contemporary Christian music band. www.tenthavenuenorth.com

Jim Rohn was a motivational speaker and author, who is regarded as one of the all-time great speakers in the personal development genre. The most impactful training I received from Jim Rohn was through his *Weekend Leadership Event* on CDs. www.jimrohn.com

Dr. Norman Vincent Peale was a minister and author. He is most widely known for his book *The Power of Positive Thinking*. This book literally changed my life and I would highly recommend it. No website available but his books are available everywhere.

Henry Ford was the founder of the Ford Motor Company and sponsor of the development of the assembly line production technique of mass production.

Les Brown is a motivational speaker and author. Something in his words just sink into my soul. His one statement, "your struggle did not come to stay but it came to pass," literally changed the trajectory of my life at a time of desperation. www.lesbrown.org

Oprah Winfrey has become a worldwide brand. www.oprah.com

Tony Robbins is a motivational speaker and author. His book *Awaken the Giant Within* was helpful when I began to bounce back. www.tonyrobbins.com

Deion Sanders is a former NFL and MLB player that was inducted into the Pro Football Hall of Fame in 2011. www.deionsanders21.com

Kirk Franklin is a gospel musician, choir director, and author. www.kirk-franklin.com

Earl Nightingale was a motivational speaker and author. He was known as the "Dean of Personal Development." www.earlnightingale.com

Sir Sydney Portier is an actor, director, author, and diplomat. His book *The Measure of a Man: A Spiritual Autobiography* is a great read.

C.S. Lewis was a novelist, poet, academic, medievalist, literary critic, essayist, lay theologian, and Christian apologist. www.cslewis.org

Robert Byrne is an author. www.byrne.org

Made in the USA
Charleston, SC
29 April 2014